House of Commons
Defence Committee

The UK deployment to Afghanistan

Fifth Report of Session 2005–06

Report, together with formal minutes, oral and written evidence

*Ordered by The House of Commons
to be printed 28 March 2006*

HC 558
Published on 6 April 2006
by authority of the House of Commons
London: The Stationery Office Limited
£14.50

The Defence Committee

The Defence Committee is appointed by the House of Commons to examine the expenditure, administration, and policy of the Ministry of Defence and its associated public bodies.

Current membership

Rt Hon James Arbuthnot MP (*Conservative, North East Hampshire*) (Chairman)
Mr David S Borrow MP (*Labour, South Ribble*)
Mr Colin Breed MP (*Liberal Democrat, South East Cornwall*)
Mr David Crausby MP (*Labour, Bolton North East*)
Linda Gilroy MP (*Labour, Plymouth Sutton*)
Mr David Hamilton MP (*Labour, Midlothian*)
Mr Mike Hancock MP (*Liberal Democrat, Portsmouth South*)
Mr Dai Havard MP (*Labour, Merthyr Tydfil and Rhymney*)
Mr Adam Holloway MP (*Conservative, Gravesham*)
Mr Brian Jenkins MP (*Labour, Tamworth*)
Mr Kevan Jones MP (*Labour, Durham North*)
Robert Key MP (*Conservative, Salisbury*)
Mr Mark Lancaster MP (*Conservative, Milton Keynes North East*)
John Smith MP (*Labour, Vale of Glamorgan*)

The following Members were also Members of the Committee during this Parliament.

Derek Conway MP (*Conservative, Old Bexley and Sidcup*)
Mr Desmond Swayne MP (*Conservative, New Forest West*)

Powers

The committee is one of the departmental select committees, the powers of which are set out in House of Commons Standing Orders, principally in SO No 152. These are available on the Internet via www.parliament.uk.

Publications

The Reports and evidence of the Committee are published by The Stationery Office by Order of the House. All publications of the Committee (including press notices) are on the Internet at:

www.parliament.uk/parliamentary_committees/defence_committee.cfm

Committee staff

The current staff of the Committee are Philippa Helme (Clerk), Richard Cooke (Second Clerk), Ian Rogers (Audit Adviser), Stephen Jones (Committee Specialist), Adrian Jenner (Inquiry Manager), Sue Monaghan (Committee Assistant), Sheryl Dinsdale (Secretary) and Stewart McIlvenna (Senior Office Clerk).

Contacts

All correspondence should be addressed to the Clerk of the Defence Committee, House of Commons, London SW1A 0AA. The telephone number for general enquiries is 020 7219 5745; the Committee's email address is defcom@parliament.uk. Media inquiries should be addressed to Jessica Bridges-Palmer on 020 7219 0724.

Cover photograph reproduced with the permission of the Ministry of Defence (www.mod.uk)

Contents

Report   *Page*

    Summary   5

1   **Introduction**   7
    Our inquiry   7
    Background   8
    International presence since 2001   8
    The UK military commitment in Afghanistan   9

2   **The ARRC leadership of ISAF**   11
    Background   11
    Purpose of ISAF Mission   11
    ISAF leadership   11
        ISAF stage 3 expansion   12
        ISAF/OEF coordination   14
        ISAF stage 4   15

3   **The UK deployment to Helmand**   16
    Background   16
    Purpose   16
    Building security and stability   17
        The UK force package   18
        The airlift and close air support package   19
        Defensive Aid Suite   20
        Threat to armoured vehicles   21
        Treatment of detainees   21
        Overstretch   22
    Counter-narcotics mission   23
        Background   23
        Narcotics trade in Helmand   24
    Reconstruction   25
    A long term commitment?   26

    Conclusions and recommendations   28

    List of Abbreviations   32

Formal minutes   33

List of witnesses   34

List of written evidence   35

Defence Committee Reports in this Parliament   36

AFGHANISTAN - Geography

Heights in metres

5000
4000
2700
1500
600
0

REFERENCE

International boundary
Main road
Secondary road
Railway (broad gauge)
Airfield • HERAT

KMS 0 — 100
MILES 0 — 100
SCALE TRUE AT LATITUDE 33° NORTH

Defence Intelligence

CHINA

TAJIKISTAN

UZBEKISTAN

TURKMENISTAN

IRAN

PAKISTAN

INDIA

DUSHANBE
ISLAMABAD

HINDU KUSH
CENTRAL HIGHLANDS

Khorog
Feyzabad
FAIZABAD
Ishkashim
Yangi Qal'eh
Taloqan
Khanabad
Kondoz
KUNDUZ
Shir Khan
Pol-e Khomri
Baghlan
KHWEJA GHAR
Dow Shi
Mazar-e Sharif
MAZAR-E SHARIF
Balkh
DEH DADI
Aybak
Kheyrabad
Termez
Keleft
Mukry
Karshi
Mary
Andkhvoy
Mari Chaq
Sheberghan
SHEBERGHAN
Sar-e Pol
Meymaneh
MEYMANEH
Charikar
BAGRAM
Mahmud-e Ragi
Mehta Lam
Asadabad
Jalalabad
JALALABAD
Landi Kotal
Peshawar
KHYBER PASS
ANJUMAN PASS
SALANG PASS
HAJI GAK PASS
HAFT PASS
FATEH BAND PASS
KABUL
KABUL INTL
Meydan Shahr
WOMAY PASS
Bamian
Panjab
Chaghcharan
Qal'eh-ye Now
SABZAK PASS
Gushgy Kushka
Towraghondi
Gonabad
Herat
HERAT
Eslam Qal'eh
Torhat-e Jam
Ghurian
Mashhad
Kowt-e Ashrow
Baraki
Pol-e 'Alam
Gardiz
GARDEZ NEW
TIREH PASS
Khowst
BATI PASS
Ghazni
Sharan
Motor
Ab-e Istagh-ye Mooqor
Qal'eh-ye Khan
Derakht-e Yahya
GHOMAL PASS
Dera Ismail Khan
Tarin Kowt
Band-e Kajaki
Gereshk
Lashkar Gah
BOST
Kandahar
KANDAHAR INTL
Spin Buldak
Chaman
KHOKJAK PASS
Quetta
Qalat
Delaram
Farah
Shindand
SHINDAND
Zaranj
Lash-e Joveyn
Zabol
Zahedan
Gowd-e Zereh
Hari Rud
Helmand
Amudarya
Murghab
Kunar
Kabul

Amey Mapping C11010/02/08/U
© Crown copyright 2006

Afghanistan: Helmand Province

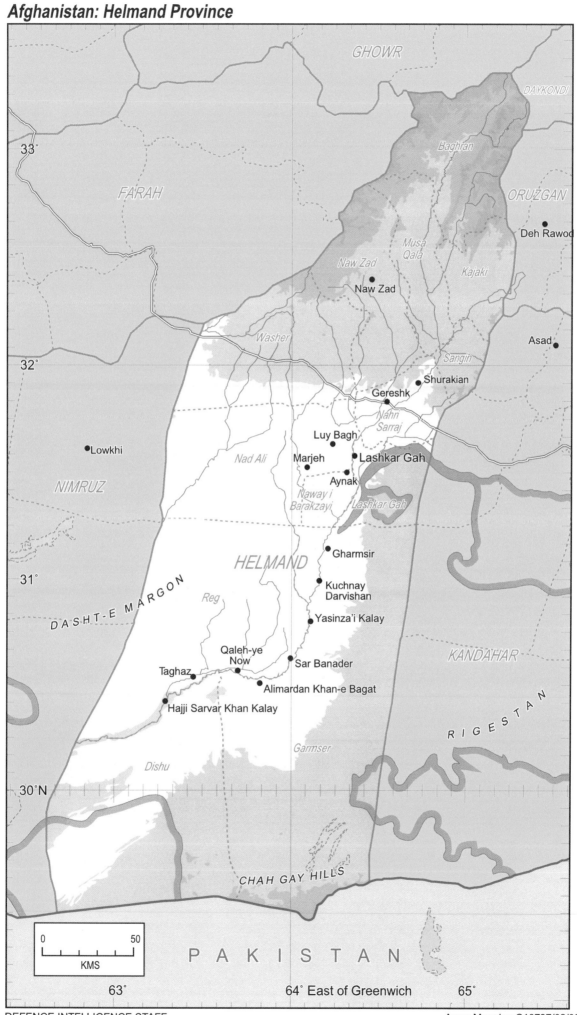

GHOWR

DAYKONDI

FARAH

ORUZGAN

33°

Baghran

Deh Rawod

Musa
Qala

Naw Zad

Kajaki

Naw Zad

Asad

Washer

Sangin

32°

Shurakian

Gereshk

Nahri
Sarraj

Luy Bagh

Lowkhi

Marjeh

Lashkar Gah

NIMRUZ

Nad Ali

Aynak

Naway i
Barakzayi

Lashkar Gah

HELMAND

Gharmsir

31°

Reg

Kuchnay
Darvishan

DASHT-E MARGON

Yasinza'i Kalay

KANDAHAR

Qaleh-ye
Now

Sar Banader

Taghaz

Alimardan Khan-e Bagat

RIGESTAN

Hajji Sarvar Khan Kalay

Garmser

Dishu

30°N

CHAH GAY HILLS

0   50

KMS

PAKISTAN

63°   64° East of Greenwich   65°

DEFENCE INTELLIGENCE STAFF

Amey Mapping C10737/02/08/U
© Crown copyright 2005

Summary

Building stability and security in Afghanistan and checking the narcotics trade, are vital objectives both for Afghanistan and for the stability of the Central Asia region.

The UK is currently involved in two military operations in Afghanistan: the US-led coalition Operation Enduring Freedom (OEF) with a counter-terrorism mission; and the NATO-led International Security Assistance Force (ISAF) with a security and stabilisation mission which will extend into the Western and Southern provinces during 2006. In due course, the ISAF and OEF missions will merge so that ISAF's authority will cover the whole of the country.

The UK is at the centre of these developments. The UK-led HQ Allied Rapid Reaction Corps (ARRC) will command ISAF from May 2006 to February 2007, a period coinciding with the expansion of ISAF's presence. This will be a crucial time for ISAF. The Southern provinces will be a testing security environment and it is vital for the future of Afghanistan and the credibility of NATO that the mission is successful. We were impressed by the professionalism of the people in the ARRC and we are confident that the ARRC will meet the challenges it faces.

From June 2006, the UK's 16 Air Assault Brigade will deploy to Helmand province as part of ISAF's stage 3 expansion. Its mission is to bring increased security and stability to the province and to check the narcotics trade. It faces significant obstacles, and the security situation is fragile. The opium trade flourishes and the livelihoods of many people rely on it. There is therefore real tension between the tasks of achieving security and reducing the opium trade. The role of UK Services in the dangerous counter-narcotics mission should be clarified.

We are deeply concerned that the UK airlift and close air support capability may not be sufficient to support the Helmand deployment. The MoD should ensure that close air support should continue to be available in Helmand, if necessary by keeping the Harrier GR7 squadron at Kandahar. We also have concerns about the effect the Helmand deployment might have on the overstretch of our Armed Forces, particularly on pinchpoint trade personnel, and we will monitor this and the other matters which have caused us concern, very closely.

1 Introduction

Our inquiry

1. At our first meeting on 21 July 2005, the Committee agreed that it should conduct an inquiry into the UK deployment to Afghanistan. Our intention was to examine the purpose of the proposed deployment of NATO's UK-led HQ Allied Rapid Reaction Corps (ARRC) to Afghanistan which was to coincide with the expansion of the ISAF mission to its Western and Southern provinces (ISAF stage 3). Our intention was also to examine the objectives of the UK deployment to Helmand province as part of the ISAF stage 3 expansion and to seek information from the Ministry of Defence (MoD) about the proposals for merging ISAF with the Operation Enduring Freedom mission.[1]

2. This has been the first stage of a two-stage inquiry, in which we have focused on pre-deployment issues for the ARRC and UK Forces deployed to Helmand province. The second stage, beginning later in 2006, will consider lessons learned from the UK deployment.

3. As part of our inquiry, we visited the Headquarters of the ARRC and units of 1 Signal Brigade, which will provide the command and control structure for the deployed headquarters of the ARRC, in Rheindahlen, Germany, on 23/24 November 2005. We also visited Permanent Joint Headquarters (PJHQ), Northwood, Middlesex, on 8 December 2005.

4. At the outset of our inquiry we held an informal seminar with Dr Shirin Akiner, Harry Bucknall, Michael Griffin, and Dr Dylan Hendrickson who shared with us their expertise on Afghanistan and the Central Asia region. We took oral evidence at Westminster on 17 January 2006 from MoD officials: Mr Martin Howard, Director General Operations Policy, and Air Vice Marshal Chris Nickols, CBE, Assistant Chief of Defence Staff (Operations). On 7 March 2006, following the conclusion of NATO's force generation process, we took oral evidence from Rt Hon Adam Ingram MP, Minister for the Armed Forces, Air Marshal Sir Glenn Torpy, Commander of Joint Operations PJHQ, Dr Roger Hutton, Director Joint Commitments Policy and Peter Holland, Head of the Afghan Drugs Inter-Departmental Unit (ADIDU).

5. We received written evidence from the Afghan Drugs Inter-Department Unit (ADIDU), the British American Security Information Council (BASIC), MoD and the Senlis Council. We are grateful to all those who provided oral and written evidence to our inquiry and assisted with our visits. We are also grateful to the specialist advisers who assisted us: Mr Paul Beaver, Professor Michael Clarke, Rear Admiral Richard Cobbold, Air Vice Marshal Professor Tony Mason, Dr Andrew Rathmell, and Brigadier Austin Thorp.

---

1   Defence Committee press notice, 21 July 2005:
     www.parliament.uk/parliamentary_committees/defence_committee/def050721no02.cfm

Background

6. Following the terrorist attacks on the World Trade Centre, New York, on 11 September 2001, Afghanistan became the centre of world attention. The USA concluded (and the UK agreed) that Afghanistan was harbouring al-Qaeda terrorists, including its leader Osama Bin Laden, and in alliance with the Afghan Northern Alliance, launched a military campaign, supported by the UK, to drive the ruling Taliban regime from power. The Taliban were defeated through a combination of US air power and ground operations by the Northern Alliance.

7. The Taliban regime fell in late 2001. Since then, the international community, through organisations including the United Nations, the G8, the World Bank, NATO and the EU, has sought to stabilise and reconstruct Afghanistan. It is the Government's view, with which we agree, that the UK has a strategic interest in bringing security and stability to Afghanistan, and it is in pursuit of this strategic interest that UK Forces operate in Afghanistan.[2]

International presence since 2001

8. The December 2001 Bonn Agreement set out a twin-track political and stabilisation process for Afghanistan. Plans were set out for nationwide presidential and parliamentary elections and an international force to ensure stability in and around the capital Kabul. The UN Security Council Resolution 1386 mandated a 5,000 strong International Security Assistance Force (ISAF) to achieve this.[3] Alongside this stabilisation force, a counter-terrorism operation was established under the US-led coalition, Operation Enduring Freedom (OEF). OEF has operated primarily in a counter-terrorism role in the South and Eastern Afghan border provinces where al-Qaeda and Taliban supporters are reported to be based.[4]

9. On 11 August 2003, NATO took command of the ISAF mission but continued to operate under the UN mandate and involve non-NATO contributor nations. In October 2003, UN Security Council Resolution 1510 paved the way for the extension of ISAF's mandate to the Northern provinces, known as ISAF stage 2. Stage 2 came into effect following NATO's Istanbul Conference of June 2004 when ISAF took command, through designated lead nations, of four Provincial Reconstruction Teams (PRTs) based in the provinces of Mazar-e-Sharif (UK), Meymana (UK), Feyzabad (Germany) and Baghlan (Netherlands).[5]

10. On 10 February 2005, the NATO Security Council announced its intention to expand the ISAF presence anti-clockwise into the Western and Southern provinces of Afghanistan.[6] Under the plan (ISAF stage 3), ISAF PRTs would be established in provinces, some of which had previously had a US presence, such as Helmand and Kandahar, and

---

2   HC Deb, 26 January 2006, col 1529

3   www.un.org/docs/scres/2001/sc2001.htm

4   www.nato.int/issues/afghanistan

5   *Ibid*

6   *Ibid*

others, in provinces such as Zabul, which had no international presence. The Security Council also agreed to increase cooperation between the ISAF "stability mission" and the US-led OEF. At the same time it was announced that the UK-led Allied Rapid Reaction Corps (ARRC) would, from May 2006 until February 2007, lead ISAF Forces. The ARRC would be commanded by Lieutenant General David Richards.

11. NATO's Operation Plan for stage 3 was announced on 8 December 2005.[7] Canada would establish a PRT in Kandahar province; the UK would take over responsibility from the US for the PRT based in Helmand province; Sweden would take over responsibility from the UK for the PRT based at Mazar-e-Sharif; and the US would establish a new ISAF PRT in Zabul province, bordering Pakistan. The force generation process, by which countries make commitments for troops and assets, continued until February 2006.

12. On 26 January 2006, the Secretary of State announced the composition of the UK force deployment to Helmand province as part of the stage 3 expansion plan. The force, totalling 3,300 personnel would be spearheaded by the 16 Air Assault Brigade of which 3rd Battalion, the Parachute Regiment is the key component.[8]

13. When, on 2 February 2006, the Dutch parliament approved the commitment of 1,400 troops to Uruzgan province in the South, the force generation package for stage 3 was complete.[9]

The UK military commitment in Afghanistan

14. MoD told us that the UK commitment to the ISAF presence before stage 3 expansion totalled "around 1,000 people".[10] This comprised:

- a PRT in the north of Afghanistan based at Mazar-e-Sharif. This was handed over to Sweden in March 2006 (the UK had handed over our responsibility for the PRT in Maymaneh to Norway on 1 September 2005);

- the Forward Support Base and Quick Reaction Force for Area North (troops which can be deployed speedily to deal with outbreaks of unrest);

- an infantry company that serves as the Kabul Patrol Company (KPC) in Kabul, and staff officers in HQ ISAF;

- UK staff officers, a training team for the Afghan National Army; and

- a detachment of six Harrier GR7 aircraft, based at Kandahar, which provide both ISAF and OEF with air support and air reconnaissance.[11]

---

7   www.nato.int/issues/afghanistan

8   HC Deb, 26 January 2006, col 1531

9   "Dutch to join British troops on mission in Afghanistan", *The Times*, 3 February 2006

10   Q 23

11   Ev 46, para 9

15. The additional commitment will comprise:

- The leadership, until February 2007, of the ISAF mission by the Allied Rapid Reaction Corps (ARRC). Including the troops of 1 Signal Brigade, this will result in an additional 900 UK troops (out of a total of ARRC contingent of 1,300) so that about 2,000 UK personnel will be in, or in support of, HQ ARRC;[12] and

- The deployment of 16 Air Assault Brigade to Helmand province and the Provincial Reconstruction Team based at Lashkar Gar, the provincial capital of Helmand. This force will comprise some 3,300 personnel.

16. MoD has told us that the UK commitment will "peak, briefly, at 5,700 before reducing to fewer than 4,700".[13]

---

12   Q 23

13   HC Deb, 26 January 2006, col 1531

2 The ARRC leadership of ISAF

Background

17. ISAF is made up of 9,000 personnel provided by 36 contributor countries, 26 of which are members of NATO.[14] MoD's first memorandum stated that ISAF was in Afghanistan at the invitation of the Afghan Government, and under the authorisation of successive United Nations Security Council Resolutions. The latest (UNSCR 1623) was agreed on 13 September 2005.[15]

18. Stage 1 of ISAF's presence was restricted to Kabul and its suburbs. Stage 2 saw ISAF expand its footprint to the Northern provinces. Stage 3, which is currently under way, will extend ISAF's presence to the West and South. ISAF stage 4 expansion will result in responsibility for the Eastern provinces transferring from the US-led coalition, OEF, to ISAF. When this will happen is uncertain.

Purpose of ISAF Mission

19. MoD described the purpose of the ISAF mission as being to:

> Prevent Afghanistan reverting to ungoverned space which could harbour terrorism; build security and Government institutions so that the progress of recent years becomes irreversible, and to enable eventual international disengagement; and, support efforts to counter the growth of narcotics production and trafficking.[16]

20. MoD regards these aims as interdependent and achievable only through the extension of the authority of the Afghan Government. On 26 January 2006, the Secretary of State told the House of Commons that:

> We cannot look to resolve just one of those issues. Everything connects. Stability depends on a viable legitimate economy. That depends on rooting out corruption and finding real alternatives to the harvesting of opium. That means helping Afghanistan to develop judicial systems, her infrastructure and the capability to govern effectively[17]

ISAF leadership

21. From 2001 to 2005, ISAF was commanded by a succession of NATO member countries on a six-monthly rotation. In September 2005 the Italians took over command from Turkey for a nine month period. They in turn hand over to the ARRC at the beginning of May 2006.

14   www.nato.int/issues/afghanistan_stage3

15   Ev 45, para 4

16   Ev 44, para 3

17   HC Deb, 26 January 2006, col 1529

22. The decision that the HQ ARRC Group would lead ISAF from May 2006 until February 2007 was announced at the NATO ministerial meeting in Istanbul in July 2004.[18] The ARRC is a NATO High Readiness Force Headquarters staffed predominantly by UK personnel with the rest drawn from other NATO countries.[19] HQ ARRC will be based in Kabul and commanded by Lieutenant General Sir David Richards. It will be supported by 1 Signal Brigade.

23. The ARRC leadership of ISAF will coincide with its Stage 3 expansion and moves to create "greater synergy" between ISAF and the OEF mission. The submission we received from the British American Security Information Council (BASIC) described the ARRC leadership as "NATO's chance to prove its mettle in the post-cold war and out-of-Europe operations through its mission in Afghanistan ISAF expansion West and South".[20] MoD shared this view, telling us that "is important that this [mission] is a success for NATO".[21]

24. Under the ARRC leadership, ISAF will have an opportunity to extend the stability it has brought to the North to the less stable Western and Southern provinces. MoD described the period of the ARRC leadership of ISAF as an opportunity for a "step change" in the international commitment to Afghanistan.[22]

25. **It is vital for the future of Afghanistan that the ISAF mission is a success. Political and economic development in Afghanistan is dependent on stability and security.**

26. **The successful completion of ISAF stage 3 expansion under the leadership of the ARRC will demonstrate NATO's value as a force for international stability beyond the geographical confines of its original Cold War remit.**

ISAF stage 3 expansion

27. NATO announced that it intended to expand ISAF authority to the Western and Southern provinces in February 2005. At the time of our first evidence session on 17 January 2006, nearly one year after this announcement, NATO's force generation process, by which NATO member countries make commitments of personnel and assets for the deployment, was still not complete.[23] Although reports in the media accurately described the UK's eventual commitment to Helmand province as early as October 2005,[24] the whole force generation process was not completed until early February 2006 when the Dutch Government announced the deployment of troops to Uruzgun province.[25]

28. It was reported that some of the delay in finalising the detail of ISAF's stage 3 expansion was caused by difficulties in NATO member countries agreeing to common rules of

---

18   Ev 46, para 10

19   www.arrc.nato.int

20   Ev 39, para 3.6

21   Q 4

22   Ev 46, para 10

23   Q 17

24   *The Daily Telegraph*, 20 October 2005

25   "Dutch to join British troops on mission in Afghanistan", *The Times*, 3 February 2006

engagement.[26] Rules of engagement set the parameters within which national forces operate and are key to determining how mission aims will be achieved. We were told by Martin Howard that:

> we never comment on the details of rules of engagement because it has operational implications, but our objective in that process would be to ensure that the rules of engagement are sufficiently robust for NATO to carry out its mission as set out in the operational plan which has been agreed by all nations. As ever with rules of engagement it will be a question of striking a balance between being able to achieve military effect but also to be working within the law and also achieving the right sort of political effect.[27]

29. NATO allows countries to exercise "national caveats" from aspects of these rules of engagement. MoD told us:

> some national contingents will have caveats on the use of their forces. What NATO is seeking to do is ensure that there are an absolute minimum number of caveats, and that is what we are seeing from the bulk of the nations.[28]

30. The exact nature of these caveats has not been made public but the Minister confirmed that they would prevent national forces participating in certain operations.[29] Despite this, the Minister was confident that caveats would pose less of a constraint than on previous NATO missions:

> I think we have learnt considerably from some of those problems in the Balkans where the national caveats really were a constraint. People who are committing [to ISAF] want to achieve the mission. I do not think they are there just for the tokenism of it.[30]

31. **We recognise that some countries have historical and constitutional reasons for not participating in certain aspects of military operations. It is important for the success of the stage 3 expansion that ISAF is able to present an effective and united front to those who seek to undermine it. Despite the Minister's assurances, we remain concerned that national caveats risk impairing the effectiveness of the ISAF mission in the Southern provinces where conditions are likely to be most challenging.**

32. **We note the Minister's assurances that national caveats would be less of a constraint in Afghanistan than they had been during the deployment to the Balkans. We recommend that MoD continue to work with NATO partners to develop robust rules of engagement with the minimum of national caveats so that further progress is made before the ISAF stage 4 expansion.**

---

26 "UK tries to form coalition to fight in Afghanistan", *The Guardian*, 15 November 2005

27 Q 58

28 Q 156

29 Q 144

30 Q 146

33. We were concerned that, should the security situation in the South require reinforcements to the deployment, the UK might be required to provide the additional forces. MoD confirmed to us that it would consider any request from NATO for further reinforcements but that NATO would have other options including the NATO Strategic Reserve Force and NATO Response Force which could be deployed "in extremis" to reinforce the Afghanistan operation.[31]

34. **We are concerned that, should the security situation in the South prove worse than anticipated, the UK will be called on to provide additional forces. The UK has already committed significant numbers of troops and assets to ISAF stage 3. NATO should call on the military assets of other countries before approaching the UK for further contributions.**

ISAF/OEF coordination

35. Stage 3 expansion will bring the ISAF security and stability mission into the Southern provinces which are currently the responsibility of the OEF counter–terrorism mission. It is possible that after stage 3 is completed, ISAF and OEF Forces will, on occasion, operate in the same geographical areas. Certain assets—notably air support—are shared. Effective coordination is therefore essential.

36. On 26 January 2006, the Secretary of State told the House of Commons that ISAF stage 3 would bring "greater synergy between ISAF and OEF" by the creation of a single NATO HQ in Afghanistan (responsible for three-quarters of the country).[32] Within this HQ there will be a three star Commander (initially Lieutenant General Sir David Richards) with three two star Officers reporting to him. Of these Officers one will be responsible for managing air assets, one for stability operations, and one (an embedded US Officer) for coordinating the remaining US Forces engaged in counter-terrorism operations.[33] The Minister told us that all NATO assets, including US-deployed NATO assets, will be commanded by the ISAF commander.[34]

37. ISAF and OEF air assets have been, and will continue to be, commanded from the air component operation centre at al Udeid in Qatar which is also responsible for allocating air assets to Operation Telic in Iraq. This air operation centre is under the command of United States Central Command (US CENTCOM). At our evidence session on 7 March 2006, we asked Air Marshal Sir Glenn Torpy whether he was satisfied that the ISAF mission would receive the air support it needed from CENTCOM. He replied "it is in the US interest to ensure that their air resources are available to support the ISAF mission which they will be".[35]

38. **We welcome the creation of a single HQ to command ISAF and OEF as a logical consequence of the increased "synergy" of the missions. On paper the command,**

31   Q 159

32   HC Deb, 26 January 2006, col 1536

33   Q 152

34   Q 153

35   Q 179

control and communication arrangements between ISAF and OEF seem clear, but the success of the arrangements will be tested when operational decisions have to be made. We will scrutinise closely the operational effectiveness of these arrangements particularly in regard to the allocation of air assets.

39. MoD states that the role of ISAF is explicitly aimed at stabilisation and not counter-terrorism. In practice, this distinction may prove theoretical. In the Southern provinces it is possible that ISAF Forces may get drawn into fighting terrorists. We were concerned that ISAF Forces should not be restricted by their rules of engagement from engaging proactively with al-Qaeda or other threats should they arise. When we pressed the Minister for assurances that UK Forces would be permitted to take offensive action against forces that are threatening them and, if necessary, pursue and destroy such forces, he told us "the answer to that would be yes".[36]

40. **We welcome the Minister's assurances that UK Forces would be permitted to take offensive action against forces that are threatening them and, if necessary, pursue and destroy such forces. In the more dangerous South, it is essential that UK commanders are empowered to act proactively against known threats.**

ISAF stage 4

41. MoD told us that NATO envisages eventually expanding the ISAF mission into the remaining Eastern provinces which are now under OEF command. We were told that ISAF stage 4 expansion into East Afghanistan envisages that OEF troops would be "re-badged" and operate under the ISAF mission.[37] It is currently unclear when this will happen although Dr Roger Hutton told us that MoD was keen for stage 4 to be completed during the ARRC leadership of ISAF.[38]

42. **MoD anticipates that ISAF stage 4 expansion will happen under the leadership of the ARRC and that OEF Forces in the East will be re-badged under ISAF command. It is important that command and control arrangements are finalised and shown to be effective before the two missions are merged.**

---

36   Q 147

37   Q 151

38   *Ibid*

3 The UK deployment to Helmand

Background

43. Helmand Province, situated in the South of Afghanistan, is a province where security is described by MoD as "less benign" than in the North.[39] UK Forces can expect to face very different conditions than they did in their Northern base at Mazar-e-Sharif. Helmand is a powerbase for supporters of the deposed Taliban regime and contains areas of significant poppy cultivation on which a long and established supply chain of farmers, traders and traffickers depend to make their living.

Purpose

44. We pressed MoD to clarify what our troops were being asked to achieve and the conditions they could expect to face once there. Martin Howard told us that the purpose of the UK deployment to Helmand Province was to:

> help build Afghan security institutions and also to assist the Afghan authorities in counter-insurgency and other stability-related activities. In the same way that that is the mission of NATO, that would be our mission within that.[40]

45. The UK is the G8 lead nation with responsibility for assisting the Government of Afghanistan in pursuing a counter-narcotics policy. MoD told us that it had chosen to deploy to Helmand Province specifically because it was an area containing continuing threats to stability from the narcotics trade, the Taliban and other illegally armed groups.[41] MoD plans, over the "medium term", to build the capacity of the Afghan National Army and Police with a view to transferring responsibility to them for countering these security threats.[42]

46. The objectives of the UK Government in Helmand are threefold:

- Enhancing stability and security through the deployment of the 16 Air Assault Brigade;

- Long term reconstruction through the Provincial Reconstruction Team based at Lashkar Gar; and

- Containment of the opium trade by working with and developing the capability of the Afghan National Army.[43]

47. **We support the objectives of the UK deployment to Helmand. UK Forces working with the Government of Afghanistan in building the capability of Afghan security institutions can bring greater security to the people of Helmand and help create the**

---

39   Ev 46, para 10

40   Q 84

41   Ev 46, para 12

42   *Ibid*

43   Ev 44, para 3

conditions for political and economic development. To achieve greater security and stability, the deployment will have to overcome significant vested interests. These threats are significant and the success of the UK deployment is by no means certain.

Building security and stability

48. At the outset of our inquiry, MoD described the security situation in the Southern provinces, including Helmand, as "less stable" than in the North, but said that there were no security challenges which posed a strategic threat to Afghanistan.[44] In early 2006, South Afghanistan experienced a series of incidents which seemed to bring this judgment into question. In February 2006, the deputy Governor of Helmand was involved in an incident when a convoy he was travelling in with Afghan National Army soldiers was overwhelmed by 200 armed Taliban. The Governor was only rescued by the intervention of Coalition troops.[45] There was an attack on US Forces in Nangahar province resulting in the deaths of four US soldiers. In March 2006, two Canadian soldiers were killed in Kandahar province by a roadside explosion and one Canadian officer was left critically ill after suffering a machete attack.[46] These incidents followed the death of a Canadian diplomat following a suicide bomb in December 2005.[47] In March 2006, there were press reports that the Taliban in Helmand had been setting schools on fire and seeking to intimidate teachers into not teaching children.[48]

49. At our second evidence session in March 2006, we suggested to the Minister that the security situation was noticeably less positive than it had been previously. The Minister replied "you are right in saying when we looked at this initially that there was a different climate than that which exists now".[49] But he maintained that "the threat level on the ground can be over-stated".[50] Asked who was responsible for the violence, the Minister described a situation where allegiances were fluid according to "who is paying them".[51]

50. MoD later described the capabilities of the Taliban and al-Qaeda in Southern Afghanistan as "limited" and stated that, "the actual numbers of Taliban in Southern Afghanistan fluctuates, but could amount to over a thousand. Al-Qaeda's presence in the area is small".[52]

51. **While we note the Minister's assurances that there are no security threats which pose a strategic threat to Afghanistan, recent events suggest that the security situation in Helmand is becoming increasingly fragile.**

---

44   Ev 44, para 3

45   "Fears for British troops as Taliban launch new attack". *The Independent*, 4 February 2006

46   www.newsvote.bbc.co.uk/mpapps/pagetools/print/news.bbc.co.uk/2/hi/south_asia

47   *Ibid*

48   "Fears of a lost generation of Afghan pupils as Taliban targets schools". *The Guardian*, 16 March

49   Q 129

50   *Ibid*

51   Q 130

52   HC Deb, 15 March 2006, col 2291W

52. **We note MoD's estimate that the Taliban in Helmand might number "over a thousand" and that allegiances were determined by "who is paying them". It is imperative that UK Forces work quickly and closely with Afghan security forces to develop a reliable intelligence picture of threats in Helmand.**

53. MoD told us that it plans to build the capacity of Afghan security forces through operational mentoring.[53] On 1 February 2006, during a speech at the Royal United Services Institute (RUSI), the Afghanistan Defence Minister, General Ibrahim Wardak announced plans for a UK-led Officer Training School in Kabul. This school would be based on the Royal Military School, Sandhurst.[54] General Wardak also announced that the Afghan National Army had reached a complement of 34,000 trained personnel against a target of 70,000 by the end of 2010.

54. We note the role that the UK contribution to the Afghan National Army Training Team, based in Kabul, has played in training non-commissioned officers. This has provided valuable experience for UK personnel in operating with Afghan Forces. It is reported that MoD plans to embed trainers in the Afghan National Army brigade deployed to Helmand province.[55] **It is essential that the legal status of embedded trainers is made clear and that all operational practices with regard to prisoners, and the rules of engagement under which the trainers will operate, are properly clarified before they are deployed. We intend to monitor these arrangements closely.**

55. **Building security will take time, and is dependent on developing the capability of Afghan Forces. We welcome MoD's plans to work closely with Afghans to develop the capability of the Afghan National Army. A well-trained army is key to bringing long-term stability to Helmand.**

The UK force package

56. On 26 January 2006, after many weeks of media speculation, the Secretary of State announced the composition of the UK deployment to Helmand province as part of the ISAF stage 3 expansion.[56] The main elements of the announcement were:

- In February 2006, a deployment of Royal Engineers and a company from 42 Commando Royal Marines would deploy to Helmand to build the encampment, known as Camp Bastion, for the main deployment;

- The Taskforce HQ and the PRT "heart" would be based at Lashkar Gar. A small company would be based at Gereshk;

- From July 2006, a 3,300-strong British force would deploy to Helmand under a new Multinational Brigade (South), initially under Canadian, then British command. The

---

53   Ev 47, para 14

54   www.rusi.org/events/ref:E43DF7B4CA8457/showpast:true/

55   Q 71

56   HC Deb, 26 January 2006, col 1531

force would comprise elements of the 16 Air Assault Brigade and an infantry battle group, based initially around the 3rd Battalion the Parachute Regiment;

- The force would include eight Apache attack helicopters (deployed on operations for the first time), four Lynx and six Chinook helicopters; and

- The UK commitment to Helmand would be for three years and would cost around £1billion over a five year period.

The airlift and close air support package

57. The size, rugged terrain and lack of passable roads in Helmand mean that air lift will be vital to move troops between locations quickly, and to resupply, reinforce and sometimes evacuate them. The deployment of air assets will continue to be coordinated from the allied air component operation centre in Qatar (see paragraph 37).

58. The airlift package in support of the 16 Air Assault Brigade, as announced by the Secretary of State on 26 January, will consist of four Lynx and six Chinook helicopters.[57] Air Marshal Torpy told us that the package would be supplemented by 20 US helicopters and "some" Dutch helicopters.[58]

59. **Given the importance to the Helmand mission of airlift capability, we note with concern the small number of UK helicopters dedicated to the deployment. We welcome the commitment made by the US and Dutch air forces to supplement the UK airlift. We remain deeply concerned about the ability of the UK's ten dedicated helicopters to perform the extensive range of roles that will be asked of them, particularly given the demanding environment in which they will operate and the likely attrition rates that will result.**

60. Close air support provided by both helicopters and fixed wing aircraft has been an integral feature of counter-insurgency and force protection operations in Afghanistan since 2001. The importance of mobile air assets was demonstrated in February 2006, when the Quick Reaction Force was dispatched in support of Norwegian ISAF troops who had come under violent attack in Maymaneh. We were told during our visit to HQ ARRC that in Afghanistan and Iraq, tasking Harrier GR7s to fly low over hostile crowds had proved effective in dispersing them without needing to fire weapons. Air support is also vital in gathering intelligence about where enemy forces are concentrated.

61. Air Marshal Torpy told us that the UK close air support package, comprising eight Apache attack helicopters and the six Harrier GR7 aircraft based at Kandahar, would be supplemented by six Dutch F16s and that the:

US have a number of A10s and out of theatre there is a range of US resources which they have committed to Afghanistan as well in terms of intelligence, surveillance,

57 HC Deb, 26 July 2006, col 1531

58 Q 178

reconnaissance aircraft, air to air refuelling aircraft and strategic aircraft such as B52s which can carry out a precision attack. Overall, there is a robust air package.[59]

62. **We note MoD's assurance that the total close air support package is robust and that the US commitment of close air support will remain following the withdrawal of US Forces from the Southern provinces. We will continue to monitor closely whether experience bears out MoD's confidence about the continued availability of air assets to the UK deployment.**

63. The Secretary of State told the House of Commons on 26 January 2006 that the Harrier GR7 squadron based at Kandahar, tasked with providing close air support to both the ISAF and OEF missions, will be withdrawn from theatre from June 2006.[60] During our visit to HQ ARRC, it was suggested that Dutch F16 aircraft might be used to replace the Harrier GR7 squadron if the runway was repaired in time. Air Marshal Torpy told us later that the runway at Kandahar was being repaired and that NATO was currently reviewing which air support assets should be based there.[61]During our visit to Strike Command in March 2006, we were told that the review was on-going.

64. **The availability of close air support providing sufficient mobility and fire power will be absolutely essential to the success of the Helmand deployment. We recommend, if no equivalent force can be provided by the NATO force generation process, that the Harrier GR7 squadron based at Kandahar should remain beyond June 2006 and for as long as necessary.**

Defensive Aid Suite

65. On 30 January 2005, a C130K Hercules was shot down in Iraq.[62] Inevitably discussion arose about the extent and effectiveness of the Defensive Aid Suite (DAS) fitted to aircraft deployed to Afghanistan. One former C130 Hercules pilot wrote to us expressing his concerns suggesting, amongst other things, that resources had been a constraint on decisions taken about the fitting of the DAS.

66. Air Marshal Torpy told the Committee that "All our aircraft will have an appropriate suite of those capabilities to match the threat that our intelligence indicates is going to be faced in Afghanistan".[63] Following the evidence session, we asked MoD to respond to the concerns that had been put to us in more detail. We had not received a substantive responsive from MoD by the end of the inquiry.

67. **We note that concerns have been raised about the appropriateness of the defensive aid suite fitted to C130 Hercules used in Afghanistan. We also note MoD's assurances that the Hercules DAS is appropriate to conditions in Afghanistan.**

---

59   Q 178

60   HC Deb, 26 January 2006, col 1532

61   Q 182

62   www.lyneham.raf.mod.uk/html/news/iraq/c130_Down.htm

63   Q 198

68. We accept that the scope for investment in equipment is infinite, but the suggestion that aircraft are not being properly protected for resource reasons is a serious one and we call on MoD to provide evidence to demonstrate that this is not the case.

Threat to armoured vehicles

69. A recent feature of insurgent activity in Afghanistan has been an increase in the use of improvised explosive devices (IEDs) against armoured vehicles. Of recent particular concern was the IED used against a US armoured "humvee" in the Southern province of Uruzgan as it was previously thought that this vehicle type could withstand attack from IEDs.[64] We sought assurances from MoD that a sufficient quantity of armoured vehicles would be available in Helmand and that they would be sufficiently armoured to withstand the threat from IEDs.

70. The Minister told us:

> what commanders seek they will be given…. What we have got to seek to do is identify the threat levels, hear what the commanders are saying through the Chain of Command and then, if remedies can be found, put those remedies in place…. If there is need for additional equipment or new protective measures then they [will be] brought forward if it can be proven that they will prove to be effective.[65]

Air Marshal Torpy added that the IED threat was "under continuous review".[66]

71. We note MoD's assurances that the force package to Helmand is fit for purpose. The threat from improvised explosive devices will need to be kept under constant review.

72. We note the Minister's commitment that commanders in theatre will be listened to and given what they need to ensure the protection of troops. We shall monitor this closely.

Treatment of detainees

73. The treatment of detainees in Iraq has been a matter of regular public concern. During our inquiry we questioned MoD about the handling of detainees in Afghanistan. We were surprised to learn that UK Forces in Afghanistan had detained individuals "on very few occasions", nor "have they passed them on to US Forces".[67] This may be because UK Forces had been based in the relatively stable North of Afghanistan and that, when the occasion to detain people had arisen, it was Afghan Forces who detained them. As UK Forces deploy to the Southern provinces, they may be more likely to encounter individuals they need to detain.

74. We asked MoD under what legal authority troops deployed under ISAF could arrest and detain individuals. MoD told us that legal authority was provided by:

---

64 www.centcom.mil/News

65 Q 169

66 Q 172

67 Ev 48, para 7

a series of United Nations Security Council Resolutions, most recently UNSCR 1623 (2005), and by agreement with the Government of Afghanistan. ISAF policy, agreed by NATO, is that individuals should be transferred to the Afghan authorities at the first opportunity and within 96 hours, or released.[68]

75. MoD told us that it was still finalising the processes that will govern the handing over of detainees to the Afghan authorities.[69] It is also negotiating a Memorandum of Understanding with the Government of Afghanistan that will set out UK expectations of the conditions in which individuals will be held and the legal process by which they will be prosecuted.[70] MoD describes Afghanistan's judicial system, which is being reformed under the G8 leadership of Italy, as rudimentary.[71]

76. MoD told us that, before soldiers were deployed to Afghanistan, they underwent "extensive training prior to deployment, designed to acclimatise them to the conditions and to hone their skills with procedures and equipment".[72] There has been no indication that this pre-deployment package, which includes cultural awareness and basic language skills presentations, includes any training regarding the responsibilities of UK troops to detainees.

77. **We call on MoD to provide greater clarity about the UK Forces' responsibilities to detainees in the period before they are handed over to Afghan security forces. It is unsatisfactory that these matters are not yet concluded.**

78. **We recommend that pre-deployment training should emphasise the responsibilities of UK soldiers to detainees under their care before they hand over responsibility to the Afghan authorities.**

79. **The MoD Memorandum of Understanding with the Government of Afghanistan must establish clearly the rights of detainees so that they are treated justly and fairly. We urge MoD to recognise that, whilst its legal responsibilities may have been discharged, its duty of care to detainees does not end once they have been handed over to the Afghan authorities, and we look to see this fully reflected in the Memorandum of Understanding.**

Overstretch

80. The reported overstretch of elements of our Armed Forces is a cause of continuing concern for this Committee and was covered in some detail in our Report on MoD's Annual Report and Accounts 2004–05.[73] We have been eager to ensure that the deployment to Afghanistan, combined with the continuing operations in Iraq, did not increase overstretch to an unacceptable level.

---

68   Ev 48, para 74

69   Ev 48, para 8

70   Ev 51, para 5

71   Q 87

72   Ev 51, para 6

73   Defence Committee, Sixth Report of Session 2005–06, *MoD Annual Report & Accounts 2004–05*, HC 822, paras 10–19

81. MoD told us that:

> In 2006, as we increase our scale of effort in Afghanistan, tour intervals are likely to breach harmony levels in some areas such as medical, intelligence, helicopter crews, logistic, provost and engineers. We continue to encourage appropriate contributions from our NATO Allies in Afghanistan in order to take some of the pressure off these areas. Overall, we judge that the impact on our planned deployment to Afghanistan and on readiness for future operations is manageable.[74]

82. The Secretary of State for Defence announced on 13 March 2006 that forces committed to Operation Telic in Iraq would be reduced to around 8,000 personnel following the next roulement due in May 2006.[75] The gradual drawdown of forces in Iraq should help balance the deployment of UK Forces to Afghanistan, but there will nonetheless be a peak in the Afghanistan deployment in 2006 which will increase pressures on manning.

83. We are particularly concerned about the pressure on certain trades and on individuals. For example, MoD has highlighted the existing pressure on army medics, intelligence operatives, helicopter crews, and linguists.[76] We also have concerns about the adequacy of MoD's management information systems which allow it monitor the pressure on its Service personnel.[77]

84. **The UK deployment to Afghanistan is likely to result in a breach of harmony guidelines in some key areas in the short term. MoD has plans to address these potential breaches by encouraging contributions from NATO partners in those trades under most pressure. Overall, we accept MoD's assurance that the impact of the Afghanistan mission on our Armed Forces is manageable. We will continue to monitor the situation.**

Counter-narcotics mission

Background

85. The opium trade affects most areas of Afghanistan but particularly the Southern provinces. Afghanistan produces 87 per cent of the world's heroin supply and the estimated $2.7 billion annual income from opium exports accounts for nearly 70 per cent of its Gross Domestic Product (GDP).[78]

86. The UK is the lead G8 country on counter-narcotics with responsibility for assisting the Government of Afghanistan in implementing its 2006 National Drugs Control Strategy. The four key priorities of this strategy are:

- Targeting the trafficker and the trade;

---

74 Ev 49, para 12

75 HC Deb, 13 March 2006, col 1151

76 Ev 49, para 12

77 See also Sixth Report, HC (2005–06) 822, para 12

78 *Drugs and Crime*, Opium Survey, United Nations Office, November 2005

- strengthening and diversifying legal rural livelihoods;

- developing effective counter-narcotics institutions; and

- reducing demand.[79]

87. Responsibility within the UK Government for delivering this strategy falls to the Afghan Inter-Departmental Drugs Unit (ADIDU), a cross-departmental body which comprises staff drawn from the Foreign and Commonwealth Office, Department for International Development, Home Office and HM Revenue and Customs.[80] MoD told us that in Helmand the focus of ADIDU activity will be on supporting Afghan institutions such as the Afghan National Army, Police and judicial system in disrupting the supply and prosecuting the traffickers of narcotics.[81]

88. Peter Holland, Head of ADIDU, told us that, alongside ADIDU, the Department for International Development spends £130m per annum on promoting alternative livelihoods to opium farmers. The scale of the task involved with promoting alternative livelihoods was illustrated when ADIDU told us that opium farmers in Helmand can potentially generate $100 per kilogramme of opium produced.[82] At our informal seminar we heard that the income obtained from poppy production could be about ten times that obtainable from any other crop.

Narcotics trade in Helmand

89. Helmand is Afghanistan's largest opium-producing province. In 2005, 26,500 hectares of land were used for poppy growing accounting for 25 per cent of Afghanistan's total production.[83] Association with the narcotics trade affects all levels of society.[84] Press reports have suggested that the Taliban were becoming involved with the narcotics trade.[85] This was supported by Peter Holland who told us "there are some indications, particularly in the South, that the Taliban have been encouraging farmers to grow poppy this year and offering them protection against law enforcement forces".[86] There is a danger that UK Forces will become the subject of attack by groups, including the Taliban, seeking to protect their interests.

90. **There is a fundamental tension between the UK's objective of promoting stability and security and its aim of implementing an effective counter-narcotics strategy. It is likely the more successful the deployment is at impeding the drugs trade, the more it will come under attack from those involved in it. In the short term at least, the security situation is likely to deteriorate.**

---

79   Ev 55, para 2

80   Ev 55, para 8

81   *Ibid*

82   Q 190

83   *Drugs and Crime*, Opium Survey, United Nations Office, November 2005

84   Q 85

85   *The Observer*, 26 Febrauary 2006

86   Q 194

91. **We were concerned to hear that the Taliban is becoming more involved with the narcotics trade in Helmand. This development is likely to increase the exposure of UK Forces to attack as it seeks to limit the opium trade in Helmand.**

92. We asked MoD whether UK Forces would be proactively seeking out drug traffickers. Mr Howard told us that the military contribution to counter-narcotics might be quite small, and he emphasised that "it will be in support of the Afghan authorities rather than the British carrying out a counter-narcotics mission on its own account".[87] **We remain uncertain of the exact role which UK Forces will be asked to play in support of the counter-narcotics strategy and call on MoD to provide clarification.**

93. An alternative approach to controlling the narcotics trade in Helmand has been proposed by the Senlis Council, an organisation which describes itself as "an international think tank established by The Network of European Foundations"[88] The Senlis Council maintains that the UK's current policy is unrealistic and will alienate farmers and those reliant on the opium trade with the danger that they will form alliances with the Taliban or other illegally armed groups. Instead, Senlis proposes licensed opium production whereby farmers would be guaranteed an income to produce opiates which could be produced licitly to make-up a shortfall in morphine and codeine supplies in the Central Asia region.

94. ADIDU described the Senlis Council's proposals as inappropriate "at this time" because there was an absence of the necessary control mechanisms to prevent opium entering the illicit market. ADIDU also noted that farmers would be likely to receive more income per kilogramme of opium produced in the illicit market compared to a regulated licit system. ADIDU told us that:

> The nearest comparable country that currently has a licit system is India. For them the greatest price that farmers receive is about $35 a kilo. In Afghanistan it is $100 per kilo.[89]

95. **We note the proposals of the Senlis Council for the licensing of opium production but we accept, in the absence of a well developed legal and security system, ADIDU's conclusion that the Senlis Council's proposals would be inappropriate at this time.**

96. **We support ADIDU's focus on developing Afghan security institutions capable of targeting drug growers and traffickers, and on encouraging farmers to pursue alternative livelihoods. However, we believe the task of controlling and reducing the amount of opium produced in Helmand, requires a long-term strategy lasting well after a secure environment has been established.**

Reconstruction

97. Reconstruction in Afghanistan is the responsibility of Provincial Reconstruction Teams (PRTs) described by MoD as "joint civil-military teams deployed to extend the influence of

---

87   Q 84

88   Ev 52, para 1

89   Q 195

the Government of Afghanistan beyond Kabul, facilitating the development of security sector reform and the reconstruction effort".[90]

98. There is no fixed template for PRTs in Afghanistan and they have tended to evolve organically in response to local conditions.[91] The UK PRT in Helmand will take over from a US-run PRT and will be based at Lashkar Gar. Like the UK's PRT based, until March 2006, in the Northern town of Mazar-e-Shariff, the Helmand PRT will concentrate on stabilisation activities in order to enable a more permissive environment for development work to take place.[92]

99. The contrasting approach to stabilisation taken by US PRTs became apparent during the course of our inquiry. During our informal seminar we were told that US PRTS had substantial funds and impressed the local population through "Quick Impact Projects".[93] We were also told that the UK PRT would have less resources at its disposal which would be concentrated on longer–term sustainable development projects. We were concerned that the disparity between the funds available to UK and US PRTs would hinder the UK's attempt to make an immediate and positive impact on the local population. In response to our concerns, MoD told us that the US has spent nearly $100 million in Helmand province and the UK planned expenditure of £38 million in the first year of deployment.[94]

100. The UK PRT, unlike the US model, intends to direct funds through the central Afghanistan Government and provincial Government. MoD regards this policy as contributing to the extension of the reach of the Afghan Government. There will be funds available for UK Commanders for small-scale local projects but these will be allocated in consultation with representatives of DFID and the FCO.[95]

101. **We note the UK's commitment of £38 million for sustainable development in the Helmand PRT's first year. We welcome the intention to commit resources through the Government of Afghanistan and provincial bodies, but call on the UK Government to put in place safeguards to ensure that those resources fully reach their intended recipients. We argue that only by involving Afghans in key decisions will reconstruction work prove to be sustainable.**

A long term commitment?

102. The Secretary of State described the UK force deployment as "formidable", but so too are the challenges it will face.[96] It is essential that the deployment should include the personnel, assets and protection it requires to fulfil its demanding objectives. It is also essential that the UK sees through the commitment it has made to Afghanistan and to its NATO allies.

---

90   Ev 45, para 6

91   *Ibid*

92   Ev 50, para 20

93   Ev 50, para 21

94   Ev 50, para 21 and Ev 52, para 9

95   Ev 52, para 11

96   HC Deb, 26 July 2006, col 1532

103. On 26 January 2006, the Secretary of State told the House of Commons that the UK commitment to Helmand was for three years. At our evidence session of 7 March 2006, the Minister was reluctant to specify an exit strategy but he told us that an exit from Helmand would be possible only after Afghan security institutions had been established and proven to be effective.[97] The Minister also said that it was in the UK's "enlightened self-interest" that the conditions that applied in Afghanistan leading up to 9 September 2001 were not allowed to return.[98]

104. **We do not believe it will prove possible to complete the reform of the security and justice institutions in Helmand within the three-year commitment so far made.**

105. **The Minister's reluctance to discuss an exit strategy from Helmand is understandable but we believe that MoD should be more forthcoming about how it will measure the success of the deployment. We recommend that MoD make public the targets by which they intend to measure the success of the Helmand deployment.**

106. This Committee intends to visit Afghanistan in the summer of 2006. We will produce a second-stage report, examining the lessons to be learnt from the deployment, in due course.

---

97   Q 136

98   *Ibid*

Conclusions and recommendations

1. It is vital for the future of Afghanistan that the ISAF mission is a success. Political and economic development in Afghanistan is dependent on stability and security. (Paragraph 25)

2. The successful completion of ISAF stage 3 expansion under the leadership of the ARRC will demonstrate NATO's value as a force for international stability beyond the geographical confines of its original Cold War remit. (Paragraph 26)

3. We recognise that some countries have historical and constitutional reasons for not participating in certain aspects of military operations. It is important for the success of the stage 3 expansion that ISAF is able to present an effective and united front to those who seek to undermine it. Despite the Minister's assurances, we remain concerned that national caveats risk impairing the effectiveness of the ISAF mission in the Southern provinces where conditions are likely to be most challenging. (Paragraph 31)

4. We note the Minister's assurances that national caveats would be less of a constraint in Afghanistan than they had been during the deployment to the Balkans. We recommend that MoD continue to work with NATO partners to develop robust rules of engagement with the minimum of national caveats so that further progress is made before the ISAF stage 4 expansion. (Paragraph 32)

5. We are concerned that, should the security situation in the South prove worse than anticipated, the UK will be called on to provide additional forces. The UK has already committed significant numbers of troops and assets to ISAF stage 3. NATO should call on the military assets of other countries before approaching the UK for further contributions. (Paragraph 34)

6. We welcome the creation of a single HQ to command ISAF and OEF as a logical consequence of the increased "synergy" of the missions. On paper the command, control and communication arrangements between ISAF and OEF seem clear, but the success of the arrangements will be tested when operational decisions have to be made. We will scrutinise closely the operational effectiveness of these arrangements particularly in regard to the allocation of air assets. (Paragraph 38)

7. We welcome the Minister's assurances that UK Forces would be permitted to take offensive action against forces that are threatening them and, if necessary, pursue and destroy such forces. In the more dangerous South, it is essential that UK commanders are empowered to act proactively against known threats. (Paragraph 40)

8. MoD anticipates that ISAF stage 4 expansion will happen under the leadership of the ARRC and that OEF Forces in the East will be re-badged under ISAF command. It is important that command and control arrangements are finalised and shown to be effective before the two missions are merged. (Paragraph 42)

9. We support the objectives of the UK deployment to Helmand. UK Forces working with the Government of Afghanistan in building the capability of Afghan security institutions can bring greater security to the people of Helmand and help create the conditions for political and economic development. To achieve greater security and stability, the deployment will have to overcome significant vested interests. These threats are significant and the success of the UK deployment is by no means certain. (Paragraph 47)

10. While we note the Minister's assurances that there are no security threats which pose a strategic threat to Afghanistan, recent events suggest that the security situation in Helmand is becoming increasingly fragile. (Paragraph 51)

11. We note MoD's estimate that the Taliban in Helmand might number "over a thousand" and that allegiances were determined by "who is paying them". It is imperative that UK Forces work quickly and closely with Afghan security forces to develop a reliable intelligence picture of threats in Helmand. (Paragraph 52)

12. It is essential that the legal status of embedded trainers is made clear and that all operational practices with regard to prisoners, and the rules of engagement under which the trainers will operate, are properly clarified before they are deployed. We intend to monitor these arrangements closely. (Paragraph 54)

13. Building security will take time, and is dependent on developing the capability of Afghan Forces. We welcome MoD's plans to work closely with Afghans to develop the capability of the Afghan National Army. A well-trained army is key to bringing long-term stability to Helmand. (Paragraph 55)

14. Given the importance to the Helmand mission of airlift capability, we note with concern the small number of UK helicopters dedicated to the deployment. We welcome the commitment made by the US and Dutch air forces to supplement the UK airlift. We remain deeply concerned about the ability of the UK's ten dedicated helicopters to perform the extensive range of roles that will be asked of them, particularly given the demanding environment in which they will operate and the likely attrition rates that will result. (Paragraph 59)

15. We note MoD's assurance that the total close air support package is robust and that the US commitment of close air support will remain following the withdrawal of US Forces from the Southern provinces. We will continue to monitor closely whether experience bears out MoD's confidence about the continued availability of air assets to the UK deployment. (Paragraph 62)

16. The availability of close air support providing sufficient mobility and fire power will be absolutely essential to the success of the Helmand deployment. We recommend, if no equivalent force can be provided by the NATO force generation process, that the Harrier GR7 squadron based at Kandahar should remain beyond June 2006 and for as long as necessary. (Paragraph 64)

17. We note that concerns have been raised about the appropriateness of the defensive aid suite fitted to C130 Hercules used in Afghanistan. We also note MoD's

assurances that the Hercules DAS is appropriate to conditions in Afghanistan. (Paragraph 67)

18. We accept that the scope for investment in equipment is infinite, but the suggestion that aircraft are not being properly protected for resource reasons is a serious one and we call on MoD to provide evidence to demonstrate that this is not the case. (Paragraph 68)

19. We note MoD's assurances that the force package to Helmand is fit for purpose. The threat from improvised explosive devices will need to be kept under constant review. (Paragraph 71)

20. We note the Minister's commitment that commanders in theatre will be listened to and given what they need to ensure the protection of troops. We shall monitor this closely. (Paragraph 72)

21. We call on MoD to provide greater clarity about the UK Forces' responsibilities to detainees in the period before they are handed over to Afghan security forces. It is unsatisfactory that these matters are not yet concluded. (Paragraph 77)

22. We recommend that pre-deployment training should emphasise the responsibilities of UK soldiers to detainees under their care before they hand over responsibility to the Afghan authorities. (Paragraph 78)

23. The MoD Memorandum of Understanding with the Government of Afghanistan must establish clearly the rights of detainees so that they are treated justly and fairly. We urge MoD to recognise that, whilst its legal responsibilities may have been discharged, its duty of care to detainees does not end once they have been handed over to the Afghan authorities, and we look to see this fully reflected in the Memorandum of Understanding. (Paragraph 79)

24. The UK deployment to Afghanistan is likely to result in a breach of harmony guidelines in some key areas in the short term. MoD has plans to address these potential breaches by encouraging contributions from NATO partners in those trades under most pressure. Overall, we accept MoD's assurance that the impact of the Afghanistan mission on our Armed Forces is manageable. We will continue to monitor the situation. (Paragraph 84)

25. There is a fundamental tension between the UK's objective of promoting stability and security and its aim of implementing an effective counter-narcotics strategy. It is likely the more successful the deployment is at impeding the drugs trade, the more it will come under attack from those involved in it. In the short term at least, the security situation is likely to deteriorate. (Paragraph 90)

26. We were concerned to hear that the Taliban is becoming more involved with the narcotics trade in Helmand. This development is likely to increase the exposure of UK Forces to attack as it seeks to limit the opium trade in Helmand. (Paragraph 91)

27. We remain uncertain of the exact role which UK Forces will be asked to play in support of the counter-narcotics strategy and call on MoD to provide clarification. (Paragraph 92)

28. We note the proposals of the Senlis Council for the licensing of opium production but we accept, in the absence of a well developed legal and security system, ADIDU's conclusion that the Senlis Council's proposals would be inappropriate at this time. (Paragraph 95)

29. We support ADIDU's focus on developing Afghan security institutions capable of targeting drug growers and traffickers, and on encouraging farmers to pursue alternative livelihoods. However, we believe the task of controlling and reducing the amount of opium produced in Helmand, requires a long-term strategy lasting well after a secure environment has been established. (Paragraph 96)

30. We note the UK's commitment of £38 million for sustainable development in the Helmand PRT's first year. We welcome the intention to commit resources through the Government of Afghanistan and provincial bodies, but call on the UK Government to put in place safeguards to ensure that those resources fully reach their intended recipients. We argue that only by involving Afghans in key decisions will reconstruction work prove to be sustainable. (Paragraph 101)

31. We do not believe it will prove possible to complete the reform of the security and justice institutions in Helmand within the three-year commitment so far made. (Paragraph 104)

32. The Minister's reluctance to discuss an exit strategy from Helmand is understandable but we believe that MoD should be more forthcoming about how it will measure the success of the deployment. We recommend that MoD make public the targets by which they intend to measure the success of the Helmand deployment. (Paragraph 105)

List of Abbreviations

ADIDU	Afghan Drugs Inter-Departmental Unit
ANA	Afghanistan National Army
ARRC	Allied Rapid Reaction Corps
BASIC	British American Security Information Council
CFC-A	Combined Forces Command-Afghanistan
GDP	Gross Domestic Product
GoA	Government of Afghanistan
IED	Improvised Explosive Device
ISAF	International Security Assistance Force
KPC	Kabul Patrol Company
MoD	Ministry of Defence
NATO	North Atlantic Treaty Organisation
OEF	Operation Enduring Freedom
PRT	Provincial Reconstruction Team
UN	United Nations
US CENTCOM	United States Central Command

Formal minutes

Tuesday 28 March 2006

[Afternoon Sitting]

Members present:

Mr James Arbuthnot, in the Chair

Mr David Crausby	Mr Dai Havard
Linda Gilroy	Mr Adam Holloway
Mr David Hamilton	Mr Brian Jenkins
Mr Mike Hancock	Robert Key

The UK deployment to Afghanistan

The Committee considered this matter.

Draft Report (The UK deployment to Afghanistan), proposed by the Chairman, brought up and read.

Ordered, That the Chairman's draft Report be read a second time, paragraph by paragraph.

Paragraphs 1 to 106 read and agreed to.

Annexes [Summary and List of Abbreviations] agreed to.

Resolved, That the Report be the Fifth Report of the Committee to the House.

Several papers were ordered to be appended to the Minutes of Evidence.

Ordered, That the Appendices to the Minutes of Evidence taken before the Committee be reported to the House.

Ordered, That the provisions of Standing Order No. 134 (select committee (reports)) be applied to the Report.

Ordered, That the Chairman do make the report to the House

[Adjourned to a day and time to be fixed by the Chairman.

List of witnesses

Tuesday 17 January 2006   *Page*

Air Vice Marshal Chris Nickols CBE, Assistant Chief of Defence Staff
(Operations), and **Mr Martin Howard,** Director General, Operational Policy,
Ministry of Defence   Ev 1

Tuesday 7 March 2006

Rt Hon Adam Ingram, a Member of the House, Minister of State for the
Armed Forces, **Air Marshal Sir Glenn Torpy KCB CBE,** Commander of Joint
Operations PJHQ, **Dr Roger Hutton,** Director Joint Commitments Policy,
Ministry of Defence, and **Mr Peter Holland,** Head of the Afghan Drugs Inter-
Departmental Unit (ADIDU), Foreign and Commonwealth Office   Ev 21

List of written evidence

1	British American Security Information Council	Ev 37
2	Ministry of Defence	
	Memorandum: British Military Operations in Afghanistan	Ev 44
	Second memorandum	Ev 47
	Third memorandum	Ev 50
3	Senlis Council	Ev 52
4	Afghan Drugs Inter-Departmental Unit (ADIDU)	Ev 54

Defence Committee Reports in this Parliament

Session 2005–06

First Report	Armed Forces Bill	HC 747 (*HC 1021*)
Second Report	Future Carrier and Joint Combat Aircraft Programmes	HC 554 (*HC 926*)
Third Report	Delivering Front Line Capability to the RAF	HC 557 (*HC 1000*)
Fourth Report	Costs of peace-keeping in Iraq and Afghanistan: Spring Supplementary Estimate 2005–06	HC 980

Government Responses to Defence Committee Reports are published as Special Reports from the Committee (or as Command Papers). They are listed above in brackets by the HC (or Cm) No. after the report they relate to.

Oral evidence

Taken before the Defence Committee

on Tuesday 17 January 2006

Members present:

Mr James Arbuthnot, in the Chair

Mr David S Borrow	Mr Mike Hancock
Mr Colin Breed	Mr Dai Havard
Mr David Crausby	Robert Key
Linda Gilroy	Mr Mark Lancaster
Mr David Hamilton	John Smith

_____

Witnesses: **Air Vice Marshal Chris Nickols CBE**, Assistant Chief of Defence Staff (Operations), and **Mr Martin Howard**, Director General, Operational Policy, Ministry of Defence, gave evidence.

Q1 Chairman: Welcome to you all to this inquiry into Afghanistan, and a particular welcome to Air Vice Marshal Nickols and Martin Howard. I wonder whether you would like to introduce yourselves and say a bit about yourselves and then we will start in on the questions about Afghanistan. Martin Howard?
Mr Howard: I am Martin Howard and I am the Director General for Operational Policy within the Ministry of Defence with responsibilities for dealing with policy relating to Afghanistan, Iraq and other areas where we commit troops at the moment. To my right is Air Vice Marshal Chris Nickols who is Assistant Chief of Defence Staff (Operations). Chris, do you want to say a bit more?
Air Vice Marshal Nickols: As Assistant Chief of Defence Operations I really sit alongside Mr Martin Howard as the military part of the team in current operations both in Iraq and Afghanistan and elsewhere where there are operations. I also have certain other functions involved in capability development across the three Services.

Q2 Chairman: Right, thank you very much. Can you start with not-too-long an answer, you will understand, but a general answer of what you think the major objectives are for the deployment of the ARRC to Afghanistan later on this year?
Mr Howard: The headquarters of the Allied Rapid Reaction Corps is being deployed in May for a period of nine months. It is one of a series of headquarters that is being deployed to command NATO's ISAF mission and in that sense it is part of a continuing process. There is currently an Italian headquarters in Afghanistan. ARRC[1] will replace it and there will be a replacement for the ARRC nine months later after the deployment in May. The key thing that we anticipate happening during that period is the further expansion of ISAF's area of responsibility into the south of Afghanistan, the so-called ISAF stage three area, which picks up five or six provinces in the south of Afghanistan. We anticipate that process will be happening both before and during the tenure of the headquarters of the ARRC being in command of

ISAF, so there will be a particular role for the ARRC in ensuring that that happens and indeed that NATO carries out its task of supporting the Afghan Government to spread its authority into other parts of Afghanistan, following stages one and two which dealt with the north and the west of Afghanistan. So in brief that is the main purpose. We can obviously expand on any of those points, Chairman, if you wish.

Q3 Chairman: Okay, so the expansion of ISAF is a key objective, with what aim in mind exactly?
Mr Howard: I think it would perhaps be worth going back to first principles about what the British policy is in Afghanistan. What we are aiming to achieve in Afghanistan is to promote a stable, legitimate Afghan Government which can exert its authority across the whole of Afghanistan. The international community is committed to that and we have seen the political process occur through the Bonn Process, which is now largely complete, which went through presidential and parliamentary elections. NATO is quite a major contributor to that because its purpose there is to work with the Afghan authorities and to work with other agencies operating inside Afghanistan to help promote that stability. The reason we want to promote stability is obviously because that is in the interests of the people of Afghanistan and in the interests of the wider international community. We are also keen to promote it because we want to reduce the risk of Afghanistan either in part or whole reverting to the kind of ungoverned space which allowed al-Qaeda to operate in a particular way during the late 1990s and the early part of this century. That is the essential context within which both NATO is carrying out its mission and we are contributing to that. It is not the only part of the international community's involvement and nor should it be. There is no military answer to this but it is an important part of promoting the stability that we all want to see.

Q4 Chairman: The British American Security Information Council has submitted a memorandum[2]

---

[1] *Note:* Allied Rapid Reaction Corps.

[2] *Note:* See Ev 37.

to us in which one NATO official is quoted as saying "Afghanistan is where NATO's credibility is on the line". Do you agree with that?

Mr Howard: I have not seen the memorandum. I think this is an extremely important issue for NATO. I think it is important for NATO as an alliance to make a success of it. So I perhaps would not put it in quite those stark terms but it is important that this is a success for NATO.

Q5 Chairman: And how will you judge whether success has been achieved?

Mr Howard: I think that what we would want to see as a result of this deployment (and perhaps I could just in parenthesis say there is of course a stage four as part of the NATO plan which would see NATO's authority extending into the south-east part of Afghanistan as well just for completeness) but the measure of success in very broad strategic terms would be that there was effective Afghan national and provincial government, and that is an important point, and that there is linkage between the two; that the extent to which there was violence and insurgency that that had been contained or indeed reduced to a minimum; that there were durable democratic institutions both with the Presidency and the Parliament; and that we would also want to see rather more than the beginning, we want to see the Afghan economy becoming more successful and of course more legitimate, which of course links across to the issue of narcotics which is a major factor in our considerations.

Q6 Chairman: Those are all judgment calls, are they not, and it is quite difficult for anyone looking at it in retrospect to have any measurable idea of whether effective government has been brought to a country like Afghanistan, it seems to me?

Mr Howard: I think that is a fair point, Chairman, a lot of this is a judgement call and it has to be a judgement call by the international community at large, but there are some things that you can measure. I mentioned the fact that elections have taken place both for the Presidency and for the Parliament, where there was a good turnout right across the country, including in the south and east, the more difficult areas. You can measure the size, training and effectiveness of the Afghan security forces. I should have said that one of the things that will be a measure of success will be the existence of effective Afghan security forces. There are something like over 50,000 policemen in the Afghan National Police and something like 28,000 in the Afghan National Army. There is still a long way to go in terms of their training, their equipment and their ability to operate across the whole of Afghanistan but a start has been made, so we would want to see the conclusion of that process.

Q7 Chairman: So a continuation with any numbers attached to that continuation?

Mr Howard: I think the issue of numbers is ultimately, of course, a matter for the Afghan Government to decide how many people they want in their Armed Forces, and they will reach that view. I

think it is still a matter of debate within the Afghan Government and between the Afghan Government and NATO and the international community who are helping provide the training. As important as numbers and perhaps possibly more important is the training that they receive and whether they are properly equipped, and also I think in the case of the Police it is very important that there is a parallel effective justice sector so that justice can be applied both at the national level and at the provincial level. So that would be another key indicator. There are some things that will be measured in that way but ultimately a lot of this rests on political judgment so your basic point is of course right.

Q8 Chairman: From whom will political direction in doing these things come? Who will the ARRC look to for that political direction?

Mr Howard: Well, the ARRC is of course the military component of NATO's role here and the ARRC will only be there for a particular period. I do not think anyone anticipates that after the nine-month ARRC deployment that all these issues that I have set out will be resolved. The ARRC will take its turn and then someone else will replace it. I think the broader question of judgment about when the international community feels that Afghanistan has reached a process of stability will be for many actors. One actor will be the Afghan Government of course; another will be the UN; others will be the G8 nations who have taken a particular line on particular issues in Afghanistan. Of course, it is unlikely to be a cliff edge. There will not be a point where Afghanistan is unstable and the next stage where it is stable. It will be a progressive process.

Q9 Chairman: The thing that worries me about this, though, is that ISAF in general seems to have so many masters that in practice it has none.

Mr Howard: I am not sure I agree entirely with that. In strictly military terms it is quite clear the Chain of Command goes from ISAF units on the ground to the headquarters in command and it will be General Sir David Richards when the ARRC takes over in May back to SACEUR[3] in Brussels. He in turn would be responsible both to the Military Committee in NATO and the North Atlantic Council which, as it were, provides the overall political cover, so I think that is fairly clear. I think there are many actors and NATO is a very significant actor, I believe, but it is not the only actor.

Chairman: Thank you. Moving on to the general security situation in Afghanistan, Mike Hancock?

Q10 Mr Hancock: Good morning, gentlemen. Could you give us an indication of what your feelings are about the general security challenges that we will be facing afterwards when they pick up overall responsibility?

Mr Howard: Perhaps I might say a few words and then I will ask Chris to fill in some of the detail. I think on the overall security situation when we sent a memorandum to you in the autumn we used the

---

[3] *Note:* Supreme Allied Commander, Europe.

phrase that it was "stable but fragile". In overall terms we still regard that as a reasonably accurate statement. We do not believe that those carrying out violence in Afghanistan, be they insurgents or informal armed groups, present a strategic threat to Afghanistan's overall stability. It does vary in different parts of Afghanistan and obviously there are trickier areas, particularly in the south and east, and there are one or two areas where we have got concern. We have seen a significant rise in the number of suicide bombings. We saw the tragic death of the Canadian diplomat and his colleagues just at the weekend and 20 Afghans were killed there. So we are monitoring that very, very closely. That trend is something that we recognise as a source of concern. I think our overall judgment at the moment remains as it was when we put forward our memorandum in the autumn, but intelligence agencies and the relevant government departments are obviously monitoring the situation very regularly and ministers are briefed regularly on the security situation. That is the overall position. Chris, do you want to say something on that?

Air Vice Marshal Nickols: I do not think I have too much to add except to say clearly the security situation varies throughout an area and you will find some areas that are quite stable where there is little threat at the time, and some areas where there is a higher threat. These tend to be geographic features or lines of communication and such like. Clearly we balance our forces to meet whatever threat we expect to see in a particular area and that is one of the things that we assess and one of the things that we do whenever we go into an area whenever we are operating in an area. So we would always assess the threat literally by the day, if you like, before we go and conduct operations in an area.

Q11 Mr Hancock: One of my follow-up questions was going to be that you wrote your submission in November, and you stick with that, and Mr Howard was unequivocal that it is still the same position, and yet the figures and the incidents do not really bear that out, do they—1,200 civilians dying in six months, 900 military or police personnel being killed and on-going insurgent activity and a resurgence of the Taliban in certain areas. I cannot see how you can say what you have said with that happening. It does not seem to give the picture of a very stable situation. Looking at media coverage out of Afghanistan recently, knowing that we were going to do this report, when I looked back over the last month's coverage there are some pretty horrendous stories about lawlessness, greater insurgent activity, and a greater public appearance of the Taliban in various guises, a rather menacing threat over the situation. Why do you not think that has changed your autumn statement?

Mr Howard: Well, I think that a lot of this was also going on in the autumn. There were problems, there were attacks, there were people being killed, and there was quite a lot of Taliban activity. Taliban activity tends to vary according to the season anyway, the weather has an impact. Perhaps I will pick up two or three points. You mentioned

lawlessness and that is a very fair point and there are areas of Afghanistan where the rule of law is rudimentary, to put it mildly, and part of the purpose of the whole ISAF construct, and indeed what the international community believe, is to try and deal with that by extending the authority of the Afghan Government, building judicial institutions, building justice institutions, building the police. That is not quite the same as the insurgency that is being carried out. This is the judgment we have at the moment. We are monitoring the situation very carefully and I have said there are areas of some concern. I have picked out the rise of suicide bombers as a particular area. We are trying to analyse what lies behind that. One analysis suggests that actually this is a deliberate change of tactic by the Taliban away from more conventional confrontation with Coalition troops where in fact they have sustained a very large number of casualties as a result of that. It may be they feel that there is an alternative way through using these suicide attacks. So maybe you are seeing a rise in that sort of activity, perhaps with a reduction in the incidence of more conventional—I will not use the term pitched battles—confrontations between Taliban forces and the Coalition. So I think that that trend is a worrying trend. It would be quite wrong of anyone to suggest otherwise. However, it has not yet caused us—and we do look at this on a pretty regular basis—to change that overall conclusion. The other point I made is whether this activity represents a strategic threat to the stability of Afghanistan. It remains our view that it does not.

Q12 Mr Hancock: But if it went down that line, similar to the situation in Iraq, the presence of our forces then becomes a hindrance to the progress rather than an assistance because the local community become the targets because they are softer and so the amount of killing and devastation wreaked on them increases because they find it harder to attack our forces or NATO forces there. What does that do, in your estimation, to the Afghan public perception of what our role is? If we cannot hunt these people down because they are now resorting to suicide attacks etc where do we fit in there?

Mr Howard: I think there are two parts to the answer to that question. Firstly, the attitude of the Afghan people towards the international military presence inside Afghanistan is broadly positive. We could let you have some figures on that. There are various research papers and we could let the Committee have the figures on that. That is rather different to Iraq where there is a more mixed attitude towards the Coalition.

Q13 Chairman: I think that would be helpful, please, if you could.

Mr Howard: We will let you have that. It will only be a sheet.

Q14 Chairman: That is fine.

Mr Howard: The second point to make is that it is very, very important as ISAF operates in Afghanistan that it does so in support of the Afghan institutions. In other words, there needs to be an Afghan face to what ISAF is supporting. What we have seen, a bit admittedly anecdotally, is where Afghan units have gone into more remote parts of Afghanistan perhaps on a counter-narcotics mission, not only have they managed to achieve success in their counter-narcotics mission, they have generally been very much welcomed by the local people as a manifestation of Afghan authority. So what we would aim to do in working inside Afghanistan on the ground with the military is to ensure that we do so in a way that is seen to be in support of the Afghan authorities. That is not a panacea but that would certainly be the general approach we would take. Where we have operated like that in the PRTs in the north of Afghanistan, admittedly in a more benign security environment, it has worked quite well.

Q15 Mr Havard: Could I just ask a supplementary on that which is really the extent to which the activities of the Pakistan Government on the border are either contributing positively or negatively to some of these manifestations. As I understood it when I was there, the Harkat are one thing, the Taliban are another, there are particular groups that are if you like bolstered at certain times or not or who are on the ground in Afghanistan and give licence to people who might come in. In other words, if the Pakistan Government is squeezing these people on the borders is that having a detrimental or a positive effect? How is that contributing?

Mr Howard: I am not sure I can put any sort of quantification on this. You are right that the Pakistani authorities, particularly in south and north Waziristan and the Pakistani Army are very actively engaged in pursuing al-Qaeda and other terrorist groups. It is possible but I have not seen any evidence of that. However, perhaps I could go back and check and see if we have got any material which we could share with the Committee that that is, as it were, squeezing terrorists across the border. I think there is a broader issue that the Afghan/Pakistan border is quite porous and it is relatively easy for all sorts of people to move backwards and forwards across parts of that border, the issue about smuggling, the issue about narcotics and within that there may well be an issue about terrorism. I have not seen any evidence that Pakistani squeezing of AQ and the Taliban inside Pakistan has squeezed terrorism or insurgency into Afghanistan.

Chairman: Moving on to the expansion to southern Afghanistan, David Crausby?

Q16 Mr Crausby: Clearly southern Afghanistan is a dangerous place so can you give us an update on the state of planning for the deployment to Afghanistan and are we ready, are we prepared for the threat?

Mr Howard: Do you mean the deployment of the ARRC, Mr Crausby, or do you mean the deployment of British forces?

Q17 Mr Crausby: Well, both will do.

Mr Howard: Chris, do you want to say something about the ARRC and I will say something about where we are on the British deployment?

Air Vice Marshal Nickols: Certainly. In terms of the ARRC then the ARRC is in its final stages of planning for deployment and clearly it goes fairly soon. It has done a number of exercises to prepare itself and still has its final exercise before it deploys and so it will be fully ready. Clearly, what the ARRC does not yet know is the final date for the stage three transfer from the current headquarters but it is prepared for it at any time once it is in place out there. In terms of the NATO plans (because of course stage three and stage four are NATO plans) the broad outline plan, the operational plan that NATO has for it is complete and is agreed by all of the nations and has been through the NAC, so that is fully agreed and that is for both stages and stage three and stage four. At the moment NATO is going through the force generation process for that plan which is a separate process by which nations assign their forces to the statement of requirement for forces to complete that plan, and that is the process that is being gone through at the moment.

Mr Howard: That is right. The UK deployment of course falls within that framework. As you know, we have already announced that it is our intention to shift the focus of British military activity from the north of Afghanistan into the south centred in Helmand province and we have already deployed people on the ground to prepare the ground. The final shape of the UK force is still being finalised and it is obviously linked to the force generation process to which Chris has referred. The Secretary of State is briefed very fully on that and I would anticipate in the hopefully not-too-distant future that he will be able to make an announcement about what the exact size and shape of the British commitment will be. In the meantime of course we are making plans as reflected by the fact we have something like 230 or 240 people already on the ground making preparations against the final decision and final announcement.

Q18 Mr Crausby: Following on from that can I just ask what will be the size of the ARRC and, more importantly, are we absolutely confident that we know what forces it will command?

Air Vice Marshal Nickols: Yes, and I will start with the second part of the question. When the ARRC deploys in May or is up and running in May and takes over from the Italian headquarters, initially it will command what the Italian headquarters it is taking over from is commanding and that is effectively the north region and the west region. At some stage it should take over the stage three, that is the southern region, and then at a further stage, probably during the ARRC's tenure, what is called stage four, which is the eastern region as well, and at the completion of stage four that is when the NATO expansion would be complete. The current plans have had expansion completed within the ARRC's nine months of command. The answer to the first part of the question on the size of the ARRC is approximately 1,350 personnel. The actual headquarters staff of the ARRC are somewhat less than half of that, the actual staff officers and planners and such like, and the reason that there are so many is because the ARRC has to take its signals brigade with it and all of its life support elements with it as well, which for a headquarters of that size commanding such a wide region takes another 700 to 800 personnel, so about 1,350 in total.

Q19 John Smith: I am not sure if this is relevant, Mr Chairman. You say that the ARRC is ready to deploy. In the preparations for that readiness and in particular in the exercises, what close support aircraft have they worked with, if any, in exercise scenarios?
Air Vice Marshal Nickols: The ARRC works with close support aircraft all the time, not just in preparations for Afghanistan. Every exercise the ARRC conducts includes working with aircraft. They have their own air organisation within the headquarters which is manned predominantly by Air Force officers so they have a lot of expertise in air matters and in integration of air into their operations, and they are very well aware obviously that that is a key part or likely to be a key part of the operations in Afghanistan.

Q20 John Smith: So it would not matter what aircraft they ended up working with if it were to be different from what they had prepared for, if they prepared for it?
Air Vice Marshal Nickols: No, in fact of course the ARRC is not just a national headquarters, it has representatives from almost all NATO nations, and in NATO exercises and in all the work that NATO does, it works multi-nationally all the time. If anything, the air environment is perhaps the most multi-national environment. If you visit a NATO exercise it is quite common to see a package of 20 aircraft made up of aircraft from five different nations. They all use the same processes and procedures, they all of course use the same language, and it has been done for 40 or 50 years very regularly.

Q21 John Smith: So it would not matter if it was F16s or Harriers?
Air Vice Marshal Nickols: No, absolutely not. As far as the ARRC is concerned, it knows the capabilities of the aircraft and the procedures and processes are NATO-wide processes and procedures so it is well used to that.

Q22 Chairman: Air Vice Marshal, you have just said that the ARRC deployment will be about 1,300. To what will that bring the total number of troops in Afghanistan from the UK?
Air Vice Marshal Nickols: Once the ARRC . . .

Q23 Chairman: Once the ARRC has deployed?
Air Vice Marshal Nickols: Well, at the moment we have around 1,000 people in Afghanistan so with the ARRC added that would be about 2,300. Clearly

when we get to the stage of deploying further forces into the stage three area that will another addition on top of that.
Mr Howard: Not all 1,300 are British. I think it is about 900 so it is around about 2,000 will be the answer when the ARRC deploys.

Q24 Chairman: Okay, so from your last answer, stage three is not considered part of the ARRC deployment?
Air Vice Marshal Nickols: No, the ARRC deployment will happen anyway because it is the next headquarters to command ISAF and it is on the roster to do that.
Chairman: Thank you. Colin Breed.

Q25 Mr Breed: Could you tell us where you expect the contributions to the ISAF deployment to the south to actually come from?
Mr Howard: Which formations?

Q26 Mr Breed: Yes.
Mr Howard: The precise ISAF force package is being put together and I do not want to pre-empt any announcement by the Secretary of State, but it will be a robust force and I think it will have a very substantial ground element because that will be necessary and it will have a substantial aviation element within it, but I do not think it is really appropriate for me to be drawn on the details of that because we have not reached final decisions.

Q27 Mr Breed: It would be true to say that this has been going on for quite some while now and we getting rather close to the deployment date as such. Have you got any indications as to when this will be finally achieved?
Mr Howard: It is linked to the force generation process that Chris talked about which is going on now. At the risk of making predictions, which is always a rash thing to do, I would hope that we would reach decisions on this within the next few weeks in a relatively short period of time. I cannot guarantee that because ultimately it is a matter for the Ministers to decide, but that is where I think we are looking to be.

Q28 Mr Breed: Can we just push you a little bit further. Do you think the Dutch are still committed to providing additional troops to this ISAF deployment?
Mr Howard: The Dutch Cabinet have made a decision to deploy and they have now written to their Parliament saying this and there is a process of parliamentary debate in the Dutch system which has to be gone through. I would not claim to be an expert on that but that process is underway, very properly. We would hope that the parliamentary part of that process would be complete by the early part of next month.

Q29 Mr Breed: Right. You said that the progress so far of our deployment has been 230 or so personnel who have been deployed down to Helmand to start the whole process. Can you tell us when you expect to be able to confirm the make-up of the British deployment in total when that actually comes about and perhaps tell us what has caused the delay in providing this further detail of this particular deployment now? As you know, we went to visit the ARRC in Germany in November and we came back with the impression of course that it is fairly important for everyone to have some feeling and understanding of what is planned because it involves our troops going to an area which we all accept is a much more difficult and potentially dangerous part of the country. Can you give us some idea of when all those decisions are going to be made?

Mr Howard: Hopefully within the same broad timescale I talked about in terms of the force generation process being completed. Obviously we have been working on this for some months, as you say, and the Secretary of State is being briefed all the time. It is an intricate process. He asks question, we give him answers. I would like to think we are coming to the culmination of that process. It would wrong for me to say that this unit is going to go or that unit is going to because (a) we have not decided and (b) it would be wrong for me to pre-empt what Mr Reid says in the House of Commons. You ask why there has been a delay. The Secretary of State has said on several occasions that for the UK deployment to go ahead he needs to be satisfied on three counts. The first is that there was a viable UK military plan that we put together and so far he has expressed himself satisfied. Obviously there are still some details to be sorted out but he is satisfied on that front. Secondly, he wants to be satisfied that the non-military part of our deployment into the south was also well-developed and working in parallel with what we are doing. He is pretty satisfied that is the case. The final condition was that there was a properly populated NATO plan. There is a NATO plan which everybody has agreed to but, as the Air Vice Marshal has pointed out, it is a question of populating the force packages within that plan. It is that process which we need to try and finalise before all three of his conditions are satisfied and then he can make a final decision and make an announcement.

Q30 Mr Havard: Can I ask a quick supplementary to that. Okay, we are satisfied with the non-military bit of the UK and we have got a set of options anyway on the British component to fill the British bit of the NATO plan. Other parts of the NATO plan are yet to be completed. Let's assume that somebody does not turn up. Are we then going to see an additional set of British troops in order to fill someone else's gaps?

Mr Howard: The force generation process is a matter for NATO and that is going on and that has happened over a period of several months. Obviously if, for whatever reason, a nation pulls out that would be a gap that NATO would have to fill and NATO would have to go to other nations. We have not reached that point. They have not come to us in any sense like that. I think it would be unhelpful to speculate in too much detail but I would have thought that we would find it quite difficult to take

on another additional task if that were the case. We have not got to the point yet and we are really looking to see how the force generation process progresses and obviously the Dutch angle, as you described it, is a factor within that.

Mr Havard: Thank you.

Chairman: Moving on then to the co-ordination of ISAF and Operation Enduring Freedom operations, John Smith?

Q31 John Smith: What do you consider to be the advantages and the disadvantages and possibly dangers of ISAF being much more closely integrated with Operation Enduring Freedom?

Mr Howard: I do not see too many disadvantages. The advantages are that you will get a clearer international community security entity within Afghanistan, one entity with which the Afghan Government can deal. I think in terms of the way the missions might evolve it will be more that the OEF components in terms of missions would move more towards ISAF than the other way round, but there is a balance to be struck. I think the advantage in political terms is that it will give a clearer, more coherent and single security authority to work with the Afghan Government and indeed with the Afghan Forces, but there are also I think military advantages and Chris may want to say something about that.

Air Vice Marshal Nickols: I think there are a number of military advantages. Clearly a single command structure not only helps you in terms of efficiencies and in terms of the number of people you have to have deployed but obviously in terms of operational unity as well. Clearly there will remain some operations outside the remit of the ISAF forces. Some American forces will still conduct counter-terrorist operations and it is expected that a senior American will hold a double hat, as we call it, for those operations which again will provide an advantage because he will also be part of the ISAF headquarters and so he will see the totality of the operations in the area.

Q32 John Smith: How do you see the co-ordination working between in particular air and ground both at a tactical level and even at a strategic level given this integrated command structure? Being aware of the past difficulties in operational environments is this going to be an improvement or is there a risk because there is a little bit of an arm's length relationship, the double-hatted nature of the deputy commander could you envisage problems, given your extensive experience?

Air Vice Marshal Nickols: No, it will improve the air Command and Control because at the moment effectively you have the OEF asking for air support and ISAF occasionally asking for air support. That of course is put together and prioritised and such like but under the new arrangements you will have a single headquarters asking for air support. Clearly one of the ways you manage the air support and the co-ordination of it is you need to have an air cell at all levels to make sure that the co-ordination works not only at the top level headquarters but all the way down to the troops on the ground where you have tactical air control parties and things like that to make sure that co-ordination works. Those are very well tried and tested procedures. They have been in place for many years and are continually improved, and I think the results in Afghanistan, where you occasionally see air support, prove that that works.

Q33 John Smith: What about General Richards's actual role, how will that work in practice given that one of his deputies will be answerable to two commands? It does not seem clear to me as a layman.
Air Vice Marshal Nickols: I think because that deputy is in headquarters then that allows everyone to see the requirement and prioritise the requirement so it is an improvement on the current situation, if you like. General Richards will be acting as a joint commander. He will have an air Command and Control organisation within his headquarters which will pass the detailed requirements for air support across to the air operations centre. The air operations centre is based in Qatar. It will have representatives from all of the nations taking part in the operations and it manages all of the air support, not only to Afghanistan but to Iraq as well.

Q34 Mr Hancock: Is that commanded by an American officer?
Air Vice Marshal Nickols: Yes, it is.

Q35 Mr Hancock: A three-star General.
Air Vice Marshal Nickols: Yes, correct.

Q36 Chairman: Do you think there would be resistance within NATO in principle to expanding into counter-terrorism?
Mr Howard: I think at the moment there would be. I think the concept of ISAF is to assist with stablisation. It is not a counter-terrorism mission in the sense it is not out there looking proactively for terrorists and going to attack them. That is not the same as dealing with insurgency in areas where NATO is operating. Clearly ISAF will have to deal with that but I think it is unlikely that NATO would move into a proactive counter-terrorist targeted set of operations. I believe that would remain largely an American responsibility with some coalition partners.

Q37 Chairman: Is that not precisely what we are talking about here?
Mr Howard: What we have at the moment in the stage four area in the east of Afghanistan (which is under Operation Enduring Freedom, the US-led Coalition) is provincial reconstruction teams operating in the same way that NATO is doing it elsewhere in Afghanistan. It is dealing with the situation on the ground inside Afghanistan so it is also dealing with the insurgency operation. It is both supporting stability and dealing with insurgency and it is also carrying out counter terrorist activities, some of which are in Afghanistan but some of which are also working with the Pakistanis across the

border, so it is that last bit of the mission that seems to me to be unlikely to come under NATO's purview.

Q38 Mr Hancock: Can I ask then what actually is General Richards in charge of or is he just the token front-man for NATO but really it is all being commanded by an American General sitting somewhere in the Arabian Gulf? If he is in command of the whole operation in Afghanistan but he does not have the last word on the use of air assets, for example, who does? The American General sitting in the Gulf?
Air Vice Marshal Nickols: Sorry, I may have given you the wrong impression. In terms of air support to ISAF the American General answers to him.
Mr Hancock: Yes, but he also answers to his superior officer sitting somewhere in the Gulf, you said. He reports to two.
John Smith: No, it is different.

Q39 Mr Hancock: Are you telling me that if the CIA requested an air strike General Richards could say no to that?
Mr Howard: We are not into that situation yet.

Q40 Mr Hancock: It is a question that possibly will come up and I want to know what the British Government's reaction would be. We have got a British General in charge of a NATO-led operation. Is he or is he not in charge of all of the air assets at the disposal of the NATO forces there and does he have the last word or is that with an American commander who would agree to a strike perpetrated by a request from the CIA, as happened last week? Would General Richards be able to say no to that request?
Mr Howard: Can I first make a point and I will get to that answer if I can. The point is that as NATO expands from stage one, stage two, stage three and ultimately into stage four whoever is in command—and it depends when stage four happens as to whether it will be David Richards who is in command—is in command of all ISAF missions and ISAF's mission is about promoting stability, it is about helping the Afghan Authority to expand its authority and supporting the Afghan Authority to deal with the insurgency. So that is that. In the sort of Command and Control construct which Chris talked about (which is only one option, it has not been decided) one of the commanders within ISAF who would be responsible to David Richards would be double-hatted through an American Chain of Command back to CENTCOM and he will be double-hatted to help support CENTCOM in terms of CENTCOM's counter-terrorism mission. This is not unique. SACEUR is a NATO commander but he is also an American national commander in Europe and he commands EUCOM. So this is not the first time that this sort of thing has happened. Clearly there will be issues about deconfliction of NATO activity and Coalition activity drawing on assets in Afghanistan. It is hard to speculate in detail about something which we are quite a long way from at this stage but if forces have been allocated to

NATO then NATO I think would have first call on them. If there were American forces, for example, who have been part of ISAF doing ISAF missions and CENTCOM wanted to use some of these for a counter-terrorism mission, they would have a link into ISAF through the American officer there to make that request and then the issue would be debated between whoever is commanding NATO or between SACEUR back in Brussels and CENTCOM. I am speculating slightly here because the precise construct would depend on circumstances, so I cannot answer the question in quite the black and white way that it has been posed.

Q41 Chairman: So while NATO would have first call it would not necessarily have a veto?
Mr Howard: I do not think it is helpful to talk in terms of vetoes. These things will have to be discussed. I think it will come up quite rarely because the missions are distinct. CENTCOM could have a mission to counter terrorism in its whole area of operation. Occasionally that may mean it might want to call on American assets which at that point were dedicated to NATO. Again that is not unusual. When we went to war in the Falklands we went to NATO and said "forces we have assigned to you we are having to withdraw" and that was a matter of debate between us and NATO, and I imagine the same thing would happen here. We are a long way away from having a precise construct that would be able to give you an answer that in circumstance A consequence B would follow.
Mr Havard: Currently we have ISAF and CFC-A[4]. What you are saying then in the new construct is we have ISAF underneath and there are two deputies—and God forbid I ask you for a wiring diagram.
Robert Key: No, no, definitely not!

Q42 Mr Havard: There are two deputies, one dealing with stabilisation and one dealing with liaison (with CFC-A presumably because CFC-A will still be in charge of the counter-terrorism operations)? The deputy in ISAF will not be in charge of counter-terrorist operations and the liaison with—
Air Vice Marshal Nickols: Counter-terrorism is not part of ISAF's mission.

Q43 Mr Havard: No, so therefore that post is not running counter-terrorism; it is a liaison relationship with CFC-A which will subsist presumably?
Mr Howard: If CFC-A still exists in that construct. As I say, do not forget we are talking here about CFC-A being part of CENTCOM.

Q44 Mr Havard: That is where the confusion comes from. Is ISAF taking control of the counter-terrorism operation? The answer I think is no.
Mr Howard: That is right.

Q45 Mr Havard: Therefore this deputy within ISAF is really only a link relationship with the rest of the American operation.

Air Vice Marshal Nickols: No, he will have ISAF tasks as well.

Q46 Mr Havard: He may well have other things to do, we have got to keep him busy, but he is not going to be in control of counter-terrorism.
Mr Howard: His important function in that respect will be the link to CENTCOM.

Q47 Mr Havard: Am I right then in terms of that general description?
Air Vice Marshal Nickols: He will be the CENTCOM commander in the field for counter-terrorism missions.

Q48 Mr Havard: He will be the in-the-field commander?
Air Vice Marshal Nickols: In the headquarters I should say, in theatre. That is the double hat.

Q49 Chairman: And Qatar is under CENTCOM command, is that right?
Air Vice Marshal Nickols: The air operation centre at Qatar is servicing more than one theatre. That is the point about the air operations because you have aircraft that could conduct operations in Afghanistan or Iraq or elsewhere because air has the sort of reach and range that it can do that. That is why you have to retain that level of command in somewhere like Qatar.

Q50 Chairman: And is it right that CENTCOM has no command relationship with SACEUR?
Mr Howard: They are separate entities. SACEUR is double-hatted as CINCEUCOM[5] so he is one of the American regional commanders as well as being SACEUR. CENTCOM is another one of the regional commanders. So there is no command relationship between CENTCOM and SACEUR as such, no.

Q51 Mr Hancock: So our man reports to one person who has no real control over the actions of his counterpart sitting in Qatar?
Mr Howard: He reports to SACEUR as part of the NATO mission.

Q52 Mr Hancock: But SACEUR has no command responsibilities to—
Air Vice Marshal Nickols: No, but he will have forces allocated to him.

Q53 John Smith: Air assets?

---

[4] *Note:* Combined Forces Command-Afghanistan.

[5] *Note:* Commander in Chief of the US European Command.

Air Vice Marshal Nickols: Just as at the moment if you look at the situation both ISAF and OEF have aircraft allocated to them with certain allocations of aircraft per day.

Q54 Mr Hancock: If you talk about air assets, could a British aircraft then under this command structure be ordered to attack a target on the say-so of the CENTCOM commander without the approval of the commander of the ISAF force?
Air Vice Marshal Nickols: No, they always have to meet UK targeting directives and UK rules of engagement before they are used in any operations and those are UK rules and UK targeting directives.
Chairman: Those were the easy questions. Now we will move on to rules of engagement, David Borrow?

Q55 Mr Borrow: Just touching on that, could you explain where we are up to in developing an agreed set of rules of engagement for ourselves, given the number of national forces involved and the need to co-ordinate those forces?
Mr Howard: Before answering that would it be helpful, just going back to the previous debate if we were to offer you a note on possible Command and Control arrangements?

Q56 Chairman: I think that would be very helpful.
Mr Howard: Because it is quite confusing and you have got various things crossing each other, I am conscious if we could get maybe on a couple of sides how it might look, that might be useful.

Q57 Chairman: I think a note would be extremely helpful.
Mr Howard: Yes, we will do that.

Q58 Chairman: And Dai Havard would particularly like a wiring diagram!
Mr Howard: Mr Borrow, I will come back to your question. The process of rules of engagement is a well-developed one within NATO and that is going on now. You will appreciate that we never comment on the details of rules of engagement because it has operational implications, but our objective in that process would be to ensure that the rules of engagement are sufficiently robust for NATO to carry out its mission as set out in the operational plan which has been agreed by all nations. As ever with rules of engagement it will be a question of striking a balance between being able to achieve military effect but also to be working within the law and also achieving the right sort of political effect and, as I said, there is a very tried and tested system which is quite complex whereby these things are done and that process is going on now. Indeed, I have not got an immediate view of exactly where we are today but I think that is also reaching a conclusion. I do not know if Chris has anything more to add.
Air Vice Marshal Nickols: No, the only thing I would perhaps add is the most common situation that we find is the situation which will be defined in rules of engagement as self-defence. Everybody has the right to self-defence at any time, so whether it be

air support, which we were just talking about, or troops on the ground most of the time in the missions that NATO will be doing the reason weapons are fired or weapons dropped from aircraft is for self-defence reasons. None of the nations would have any problem whatsoever with signing up to that because it is international law if you like. The wider consideration we were talking about counter-terrorist operations is where slightly more robust rules of engagement might be required but clearly, as we discussed, that is not part of the ISAF mission.

Q59 Mr Borrow: So it would be wrong for me to assume or this Committee to assume that an ISAF force made up of a different mixture of national forces would have a different effectiveness depending upon the rules of engagement of those different national forces? Are you saying that the fact that it is a multi-national force means that the fact that there may be different rules of engagement will not actually have any impact on the effectiveness of the force as a whole?
Mr Howard: I think the objective in all these things is for all the contributing nations to sign up to a single set of rules of engagement developed through the NATO process which we have talked about. Indeed that will be SACEUR's objective and that is what he will be trying to achieve. The reality is there will always be some national caveats, not necessarily on the rules of engagement, they may be of a different type, and that will have an impact on that. That is the nature of multi national operations. The default where we are trying to get to is a single set of rules of engagement that we all follow, and where there are caveats they are very clearly visible and understood so that any deconfliction can take place.

Q60 Mr Borrow: Would it be right to say that because UK forces have traditionally taken a more robust approach to rules of engagement and perhaps been more prepared to put themselves in harm's way that in the ISAF force as a whole UK forces are more likely to find themselves in dangerous situations than perhaps the forces of certain other multi-national partners within that force? Would that be a reasonable assumption for the Committee to make?
Mr Howard: I think we should be careful about generalisations. First of all, it is not just a question of rules of engagement; rules of engagement is just one part of it. The other part is national doctrine and tactics and we have a British approach to some aspects of doctrine which will be different from others. Some nations may have a more cautious approach in terms of their doctrine but, equally, I think others would be pretty robust and I would anticipate that several of the other NATO members that we are working with would also want to be, as it were, proactive in carrying out their mission. Indeed, I am sure that SACEUR and the commander of ISAF and the commanders of the brigade in the south will want to encourage that.

Q61 Robert Key: Can I ask quickly which countries you would be prepared to name as being as keen as Britain?

Mr Howard: I do not think it is helpful to actually name countries.

Robert Key: Well I do. What about the rest of my colleagues?

Mr Hancock: That is right, yes, because if not we go to the situation that happened in the Balkans[6], do we not, where the rules of engagement were different and the Dutch military are suffering the consequences of that. They had not signed up to a common agreement on rules of engagement and had there been other soldiers there than Dutch soldiers the reaction would have been different and the national pride of the Dutch would not have been so devastated by the events that happened in the incidents there.

Q62 Chairman: Do you want to comment on that, Mr Howard?

Mr Howard: I am not sure I do. I really do not think it is appropriate for me to identify countries.

Q63 Chairman: Hold on, allow him to answer.

Mr Howard: I do not think it is appropriate for me to say that country X will have a less or more robust attitude towards activities, whether we are talking about rules of engagement or whether we are talking about doctrine. The idea will be to work through NATO processes to produce a plan, which we have, and a force package in support of that plan which can achieve NATO's objectives. I think it would be wrong for me to name country X as being someone which would be prepared to do this or that.

Q64 Chairman: Is not the key to this not necessarily that one country is strong and another country is less strong, but the fact that there are differences in the rules of engagement? Does that not add huge complications to the work that British troops have to do on the ground?

Mr Howard: I would agree it is a factor. I would repeat that it is not just rules of engagement. As I have said, the idea is for people to work to a single set of rules of engagement. Within those rules of engagement, the way you operate on the ground is very different. It is as much to do with doctrine and what the commander wants to achieve. It is a complicating factor but it is not the first time we have faced complicating factors. In every coalition operation, whether it is a NATO operation or whether it is an ad hoc coalition operation, there are issues about how different nations approach British activity.[7] It happened in the First Gulf War; it happened in the most recent Gulf War. As I think Mr Hancock said, it happened in the Balkans.[8] I am not trying to minimise the problems but we are quite used to dealing with them because over the years most of the operations we have carried out have been multi-national in character, either through NATO,

through the EU for example now in Bosnia, or on an ad hoc basis. We have mechanisms for dealing with it.

Q65 Mr Borrow: What concerns me is that I would imagine the British public will once again assume that it is our forces that will end up doing the most dangerous missions, while the forces of some of our allies, if you like, have the easy options and do not take part in the dangerous missions. Am I wrong in that assumption and would the UK public be wrong in that assumption?

Air Vice Marshal Chris Nickols: I think, if you look at the stage three area and look at threat assessments of the various provinces in the stage three area, Helmand is probably no worse, and probably no better either, than some of the other provinces. I think that would be a false assumption, yes. If other nations are filling some of those other provinces, they are going into as high a threat level or threat environment as the UK is.

Q66 Chairman: Helmand is no worse than some of the other provinces, you say, but it is worse, surely, than the provinces in which we are currently deployed, is it not?

Air Vice Marshal Chris Nickols: In the north; overall I think our threat assessments will be that the north is more benign than the south, yes. In terms of the south, and nations which may be contributing to the south, then many of the provinces are very similar in terms of threat assessment.

Q67 Chairman: So the whole danger level will increase in the south?

Air Vice Marshal Chris Nickols: Compared with the north, yes, I would agree with that. The threat assessments are higher for the south.

Q68 Mr Hancock: I have two further small questions on the rules of engagement, if I may. CENTCOM presumably do not sign up for NATO rules of engagement; they have their own.

Mr Howard: Indeed, CENTCOM is an American national command. It will operate to US national rules of engagement.

Q69 Mr Hancock: Yes, but NATO troops will not have common rules of engagement. They vary from nationality to nationality or are you contemplating that there will be rules of engagement which will be common? If I was a British commander in the field and I was being supported by another nationality, would I be posed with a situation where I could do certain things but my colleague commander of the second unit would not be able to engage, leaving the British to take a different position than, say, his Dutch colleagues? That is a real issue because of what has happened in the past.

Mr Howard: I go back to what I said earlier, which is that NATO is striving to produce a single set of rules of engagement for all the nations participating in ISAF and that would include US forces participating. They would sign up to that, as would we. It is not impossible that that there would be some

---

[6] *Note:* Mr Hancock was, in fact, referring to the Falklands, not the Balkans.

[7] *Note by Witness:* It is in fact, how different nations approach military activity, not British activity.

[8] *Note by Witness:* Mr Hancock was in fact, referring to the Falklands, not the Balkans.

modifications for particular nations around the edges of that, but the basic core or the rules of engagement for ISAF will be a NATO rules of engagement profile, which is how we describe it. The issue of how different nations operate I think in many ways is less to do with rules of engagement and more to do with doctrine. If you take, for example, rules of engagement to do with self-defence, they could be exactly the same for one particular unit as for another unit. In terms of what they might actually face on the ground, it will depend on whether that unit is actually out patrolling on the streets or sitting in its garrison. The rules of engagement will be exactly the same. It depends on their doctrine and what they are doing and what they are ordered to do by the NATO command chain.

Q70 Mr Havard: I would love to pursue this a bit further but we need to ask you a couple of other things about practical operations on the ground. It is straining the rules of engagement in a sense or behaviours, doctrine, whatever you call it. I visited the Afghan National Army training centre again in November. I saw what work was going on there in terms of what the British were doing and others. The Afghan National Army component is growing. Trained personnel are now being deployed. You raised an interesting question about the support they have to be deployed, which is a big issue we cannot deal with today. Where they are deployed, they are practical; they are being used alongside Americans, particularly the US, and they are fighting with them. The way they do that, as I understand it, is that they have embedded trainers with them who fight with them. The British in Helmand would presumably have components of the Afghan National Army to assist them in some fashion. I want to know how it is that arrangement is going to be run. If they are doing joint operations, whether it be interdict operations or narcotics or whatever, are we going to take a similar approach or effectively do embedded trainers become their officers/NCOs and continuing mentors actually fighting with them on the ground, or are we going to use them in a different way? What are those rules for the British as to how they use the Afghan national component?

Mr Howard: I will ask Chris to come in on some of the detail but the basic point is that there will be an Afghan brigade headquarters plus one or two battalions moving into Helmand in March. That will be the Afghan National Army authority there. Could I perhaps slightly turn what you said round on its head, Mr Havard, and say that in a sense we are there in support of them rather than them being in support of us.

Q71 Mr Havard: All right, but they are working together?

Mr Howard: Yes, they are working together, and we will certainly work together in operations. We would see an important part of our function, like the rest of ISAF, as developing the capability. There is a variety of ways of doing that. I do not know if Chris wants to say the kinds of things that we anticipate doing.

Air Vice Marshal Chris Nickols: We do anticipate having people embedded, at least for training tasks. We have not yet addressed precisely the tactics of how we would fight with them, but it is essentially in a supporting role. It needs to have an Afghan face, particularly for areas such as counter-narcotics and things like that. So it would be much more of a supporting function. As Martin has said, the first Afghan National Army brigade should be moving into the Helmand area in around March. It will not be a full brigade at that stage. We are expecting probably the brigade headquarters plus one of what is called its kandacs, which is broadly the same as an infantry battalion for us or a light infantry battalion, possibly two, we are not quite sure yet. There will be an Afghan National Army element there in place by Easter time this year for us to work with.

Q72 Mr Havard: Part of the reason I ask the question is not only on the operational capability side of it but also as to the situation for the British troops and clarity about their status in all of that because quite clearly legal constraints apply. They come through all the rules of engagement and all the other things that they have. I think we would appreciate some further description at some point about exactly what is going on there to put to rest, if you like, that there are not particular arrangements that need to be made to give that clarity, both to the individuals who are doing it and also to the public that they are engaging in an activity that does not put them into a different form of difficulties.

Air Vice Marshal Chris Nickols: One thing we can say, while the precise arrangements of how training personnel are engaged are not finalised yet, is that we would never put our training personnel in a position where they were at greater threat than they would be if they were in a UK unit.

Q73 Mr Havard: My other question in a sense has a similar root, which is to do with prisoners and people who are arrested during various operations. Obviously, there has been a lot of talk about rendition and rendition policies and people being oiked out of Afghanistan and flown off to Guantanamo Bay or wherever. Could you perhaps say what the situation is for all UK forces when they are in a situation where, say, they are in a joint operation with Afghan National Army people in a policing operation; they actually stop the vehicle, for example, and arrest the people. What happens to them? If they are operating independently and they come across people that they have to arrest in some fashion, what happens to these people? Where do they go?

Mr Howard: That is an issue which again NATO as a whole has to address. It is not just a British point. We are discussing that with NATO. The basic principle, because we are operating inside Afghanistan where there is a sovereign Afghan Government, is that you would want to pass those people who have been detained to the Afghan authorities. There may be practical issues about whether that can be done quickly or if it will take a bit of time. The basic approach will be to do that.

Part of the policy is to try to establish this kind of requirement when we actually move in. The basic principle will be to pass those people to the Afghan authorities.

Q74 Mr Havard: That would be the instruction to the British forces, that they should pass them over appropriately when practical?
Mr Howard: I think the instruction will be a bit more complicated than that but that will be the essential aim of what we are trying to do.

Q75 Chairman: If there were a suspicion or a belief that the Afghan authorities would pass them on to the United States and that they might end up in Guantanamo Bay, would that affect the view as to whether these people should be passed to the Afghan authorities?
Mr Howard: One of the things that we would have to do is reach an agreement with the Afghan authorities about what happens to people we pass over to them, in the same way that we have reached agreements with the Iraqi Government, when we make points, for example, about the death penalty. One of the things we would need to reach is that kind of agreement. That would include issues about how they are treated. I am not sure we could say there would be a blanket ban on them passing them on because in many ways that will also depend on extradition treaties that the Afghan authorities have with the United States.

Q76 Mr Hancock: The Americans have yet to use that extradition treaty.
Mr Howard: I am just saying that will be a factor, and also, the nature of any offence, if the individual concerned has carried out an offence, and if it involves an American citizen. I do not think we can say that we would not pass people over if they were going to be passing them to the Americans, but we would need to reach an agreement with the Afghan authorities about what happens to people who are passed to them.

Q77 Chairman: We are already operating in north Afghanistan. Do we have an agreement with the Americans that anybody we hand over to the Afghanistanis should not be passed to Guantanamo Bay?
Mr Howard: I do not think we have an agreement in those terms. I can go back and check to see what the precise position is.
Chairman: It would be helpful if you could do that because the Prime Minister has said that Guantanamo Bay is an anomaly which should come to an end.

Q78 Mr Hamilton: We have been there several years. You indicated a moment ago that we would look for an agreement. Surely, as we have been there for several years, we must have an agreement at the present time about what we would do with people of other nationalities arrested by British troops? Surely, being mindful of the British position on

Guantanamo Bay, it would be inappropriate for British troops to transfer people who are not of Afghan descent across to the authorities?
Mr Howard: I would have to check whether there are any particular arrangements already in place for forces which are operating in south Afghanistan. It is worth making the point that we have only really recently established a properly formulated, democratically elected Afghan Government, so for a long part of that time there was not any authority that you could deal with. That is part of it. I will let you have a note on this issue.
Chairman: I find it a bit odd that you cannot answer that question.

Q79 Mr Hancock: That is in particular after what you said about it at the beginning, Mr Howard, that NATO had signed up for this and that the NATO Council had agreed the formation and the rules for going into Afghanistan. Are you seriously saying that the American policy of moving from the country any non-citizen of that country who was involved in insurgency would be seen as their being able to deal with a prisoner as opposed to a national of Afghanistan who might be involved? The question is: if they suspected one of the people you had taken into your control was a possible al-Qaeda suspect, according to America, would they immediately be transferred to the Americans?
Mr Howard: I think there are two separate points here. The point I was trying to address primarily was our responsibility if, for any reason, we detained people, and that they are either released or passed across to the relevant Afghan authorities. There is a different issue about people who we detain by whatever means who get into the hands of the Americans and end up in Guantanamo.

Q80 Mr Hancock: No. My question is on what you said right at the beginning, that they had all been through the political processes within NATO; all member countries of NATO had now signed up at the NATO Council on the way in which this operation is going to be run. Our question is simply: did that include the way prisoners who were taken into captivity by ISAF forces would be treated—yes or no?
Mr Howard: I would have to check on the detail and come back to you on that. The basic principle that they might be released or passed across to the Afghan authorities I think is firm.
Mr Hancock: I am really surprised, Mr Howard, that you do not know that.

Q81 Mr Havard: Can I just be clear. I do not want it claimed later that I said something you did not understand. My question in a sense is in two parts. There is the question about what happens with NATO but there are the British forces that are operating and British forces operate in two ways, do they not? They operate with ISAF but they also operate as part of the counter-terrorism coalition. If, for example, people we do not speak about like our

special forces as part of a counter-terrorism operation actually arrest people, they pass them into the Afghan process.
Mr Howard: Or they would be released.

Q82 Mr Havard: In exactly the same way as British service personnel would do if they arrested someone wearing their ISAF badge?
Mr Howard: That would be how it would work, yes.

Q83 Mr Hancock: Is it?
Mr Howard: It has not really happened very much, but the basic idea would be that if we pick someone up, they would be either be released or if we felt that for some reason—The only reason we would pass them to the Afghan authorities, and perhaps I can be clear about this, is if, on the face of it, they had committed some sort of criminal offence and the Afghan authorities would need to do something. If they have not, then I think the option would be to release them. The difference between Afghanistan and Iraq is that in Iraq we have a United Nations Security Council resolution, a succession of Security Council resolutions which allow us to detain people who represent an imperative threat to security. As far as I know, and I am pretty sure about this, there is no equivalent Security Council resolution in relation to Afghanistan, and so the choice lies, if you pick someone up and there is an issue and on the face of it they have committed an offence, they should be passed to the Afghans. In all other respects, once the security situation in which they have been picked up has been resolved, then you would anticipate they would be released. I think we do owe you a note on this to clarify it with more detail.
Chairman: A note would be helpful. It may well be that we will need to have a further evidence session on Afghanistan, once things become clearer in relation to the NATO raising of forces. Can we move on to the purpose of the UK's deployment in Helmand.

Q84 Linda Gilroy: I wonder if you could tell us a bit more, and you have already covered some of this in the earlier questions, about the purpose of the UK deployment to Helmand, the balance between whether it is providing security and stability and the degree to which it will involves proactively seeking out Taliban fighters or drug traffickers?
Mr Howard: As you say, Ms Gilroy, at the beginning I said that the UK deployment is part of the NATO deployment. We would see it as being allied with NATO objectives, which is, as I say, to promote the effectiveness and authority of the Afghan Government to help build Afghan security institutions and also to assist the Afghan authorities in counter-insurgency and other stability-related activities. In the same way that that is the mission of NATO, that would be our mission within that. That is what we would be doing when we deploy into Helmand. It is very important that this is not seen just as a military activity. I said earlier on that we are very keen that there is also a non-military component to British activity in the south of Afghanistan. That is being developed, so that what

we do in support of the Afghan authorities on stabilisation and the military side, if I can put it that way, needs to be coherent with what we are doing on reconstruction, the development of alternative livelihoods for those who perhaps are involved in poppy growth. You specifically raised the issue of counter-narcotics. I think this is an important point. Perhaps in the past there has been a slight tendency to see the narcotics issue as a separate criminal issue, which is serious but is not part of the overall mission. We have moved on from that and there is a general acceptance that if our objective is to promote the stability of Afghanistan, for the reasons which I set out earlier on, then as part of that you do need to deal with the narcotics issue and support the Afghan Government in dealing with the narcotics issue. The military contribution to that may be quite small because the most effective contribution to that could be the generation of alternative livelihoods and ensuring, for example, that there is a justice system into which those who are caught can go and be appropriately punished. That has been a problem in Afghanistan. I would anticipate, and again this is set out in the NATO operational plan, that the military involvement would be in support the Afghan authorities' activities in this sphere. That could be, as it were, providing general security; it could be in support of Afghan-led interdiction operations. Some of this sort of stuff is happening already but we will obviously see more of it. I think the point I would emphasise is that it will be in support of the Afghan authorities rather than the British carrying out a counter-narcotics mission on its own account.

Q85 Mr Hancock: I think Mr Key might be coming on to some further questions about narcotics in due course. Can I stick with the security issues? What current assessment have you made of whether there is an effective political strategy to counter corruption in the Afghan Government and judiciary?
Mr Howard: I am not well placed to answer that comprehensively across the board. Perhaps I can tell you a little bit about narcotics. President Karzai claims that one of his top priorities is to deal with this issue. He has formed a ministry with a narcotics minister. He has set up a special tribunal based in Kabul to deal with traffickers. He has encouraged governors to promote eradication schemes. Interestingly, I think during 2005 poppy production in Nangarhar was reduced by something like 90%, mainly because the governor there had carried out a proactive eradication campaign, supported by the government. There is clearly a lot more to do. Helmand, for example, is a major area of poppy cultivation. The most recent development on that front has been that President Karzai has removed the governor, Sher Mohammed Akhundzada—there is some allegations that there were linkages to narcotics—and replaced him with Engineer Daoud, who is different. He has taken a number of steps but there is still a long way to go. It is beholden on the international community to help the Afghan authorities to do that.

Q86 Linda Gilroy: I am sure you will appreciate the importance of what I am saying. There is not much point in you getting to grips with that aspect of it if, as I think you described it earlier in this session, the rule of law is rudimentary, if there are not effective Afghan institutions to deal with these issues and follow them through properly. Although I appreciate this is not something you are expert in, you must have some knowledge of the degree of confidence that you and others can have that if you do that bit of the work, it will be followed through properly.

Mr Howard: You are right to say that I am not a particular expert in these fields. I have talked about some of the steps that have been taken on the narcotics front. I think more generally President Karzai has been keen to discourage what might be called warlordism by removing Fahim Khan in the north and moving Ismail Khan in the west and gradually extending his authority. There is a number of things that need to be done. I think the most important would be the establishment of a clean, effective justice sector into which an effective police force can link so that people who do commit crimes can be passed on. There is a wider issue of corruption. I am not sure I am very well placed to answer on that. That is really something on which you might want to ask my colleagues at the Foreign Office to give you a view.

Q87 Linda Gilroy: I am sure you are right. May I conclude by saying that it is a bit like the prisoner issue we were talking about just now. You described how the key mission is to establish and back up the Afghan Government in establishing institutions. I would have thought that there would have been some clarity on the part of MoD as to what degree of confidence you could have that in going into Helmand there would be a court process into which you could send people that you catch or support the Afghan security forces in catching in this process. If that does not exist, then it is a bit of a catch 22 situation, is it not?

Mr Howard: I think what we need to do is help the Afghan authorities to develop it as we move in. When I talked about it being rudimentary, I meant in places like Helmand. It is not something you can build overnight, but I think the fact that President Karzai has been prepared to remove a governor regarded as being corrupt is a step in the right direction. There is a lot more to do in terms of establishing local systems of justice and local provincial government. It will be important that on the military side we carry out our activities in parallel with the development of those activities.

Q88 Mr Hancock: I am slightly at a loss to understand some of the answers you are giving, Mr Howard, about the situation there because the removal of somebody who is a governor from office when in the past he has been one of the warlords does not remove him from his ability to cause a lot of problems for the area and for British troops when they arrive. I would like to be sure that we have the right sort of intelligence and evidence to show what

sort of public reaction there is going to be to the arrival of British troops in Helmand in an area where the Taliban was extremely strong in the past, who did sort the problem of poppy cultivation out in their own way, but it is now back. With the resurgence of the Taliban in that area, according to media reports, it is now one of the hot spots of Taliban activity. I would like to know what evidence you have to support the view that British troops, when they arrive in this sector, will both be welcomed by the people of that area and that they will not be confronted with a dispossessed governor who has been put out of power but his well armed band of renegades is still there waiting and willing to do whatever somebody is prepared to pay them to do.

Mr Howard: Part of the answer is that we have conducted surveys in that part of Afghanistan about the attitude towards coalition forces. I have already promised you a note on that and, hopefully, that will help to answer part of the question. Obviously one of our key intelligence requirements is to establish the attitude of a whole range of actors towards the British presence. You point out that you need intelligence to tell you, as it were, what Joe Public thinks. To an extent you can ask them, but views about the attitudes of those perhaps engaged in criminal activity, those engaged in insurgency, those engaged in narcotics, would be a clear intelligence target for us. Our intelligence agencies work very hard to get that information. As I say, we review it all the time. In the case of the governor, I think what actually has happened is that President Karzai has brought him to Kabul and given him a different sort of post. He has taken him away from being governor in Helmand. There is a new governor. Clearly, it is in our interests that he establishes himself as both an effective governor and as a force of stability.

Q89 Mr Hancock: What evidence do you have about the resurgence of the Taliban in that area? It was an area where they were particularly strong and it is an area where they are coming back, according to local media reports that I have read in the last month. Are you satisfied that the Taliban are in such small quantities there that they do not present themselves as a significant risk or is it one of the big issues that British forces will have to tackle, this tracking down of the remnants of the resurgence of the Taliban who are having a greater influence over what is happening in the area?

Mr Howard: As I said at the beginning, I think it is a source of concern. We have seen an upsurge in a particular type of attack. I should say that is not just in Helmand. I think the attacks which have been most serious were in Kandahar. Nevertheless, we are all part of NATO's ISAF stage three area, which includes Kandahar and Helmand, and other provinces as well. Yes, we are concerned about that. This is still a series of relatively isolated incidents rather than a very wide spread campaign of the sort you are seeing in some areas of Iraq. There is a huge difference between those two. But we are concerned if this represents a trend and if it is going to get worse. Certainly, we would anticipate that British troops operating in the stage three area along with other NATO troops operating in the same area would need to support the Afghan authorities in dealing with a range of, if I can call them this, insurgents, which would include the Taliban but might also include other much more informal armed groups who perhaps are carrying out attacks for more criminal reasons, or maybe even linked to narcotics. There is a range of people who may be motivated to carry out violence against ISAF troops.

Q90 Mr Hancock: I would like to be clear: In this instance, from all I have read, the suggestion is that the problem would not be insurgence from outside of the country but it would be a re-emergence of hard line Taliban taking the issue back to the local population and to the authorities of President Karzai.
Mr Howard: I do not think I said the insurgents would come from outside the country.

Q91 Mr Hancock: The word "insurgent" I think conjures up the view that these people have come from outside.
Mr Howard: I see. Then perhaps we need to be clear in our terminology. I use "insurgent" in the terms of someone who is largely indigenous in the area where we are operating. As it happens, as I said earlier, this is at the border between that part of Afghanistan and Pakistan. You could easily anticipate that some individuals, including those who carry out violence, might be Taliban moving backwards and forwards. I had not meant to imply that any insurgency was externally directed particularly.

Q92 Chairman: What you were talking about in relation to attacks was in answer relating to the symptoms of potential support for the Taliban rather than for the underlying condition. Do you believe that there is a growing resurgence of support for the Taliban or are you unable to answer that?
Mr Howard: I do not have any facts and figures. I have not seen the evidence in the last 12 months of popular support for the Taliban rising. We have seen evidence of spikes of activity by the Taliban, but that is a different thing. I have seen no evidence that the population is turning back to the Taliban.

Q93 Chairman: Are you looking for evidence?
Mr Howard: It is always something that we would keep an eye out for. If you wish, I will check back to see if there is anything over the last 12 months that has pointed to that, but I have seen no evidence— and occasionally I sit on the Joint Intelligence Committee—that that is the case.

Q94 Linda Gilroy: Who is benefiting from the proceeds of the opium crop in that area? The farmers only get a tiny amount of it. Where is the money from that going?
Mr Howard: I do not think I can give you a complete answer.

Q95 Mr Havard: Have a go.
Mr Howard: Inside Afghanistan it will be going to those key traffickers.

Q96 Linda Gilroy: Is that related to the Taliban or is it going to the former warlord?
Mr Howard: We have never seen the evidence of direct linkages between those who carry out narcotics and the Taliban. We do look for that all the time.

Q97 Linda Gilroy: So the former governor who has been deposed?
Mr Howard: I think there is some allegation that he was involved in narcotics. That is not the same as saying he was involved with the Taliban.

Q98 Linda Gilroy: This is really at the core of the whole mission. It is fuelling 60% of the economy, we are led to understand, in Afghanistan. We are told some of that may be beginning to go into the more legal economy, but there must be some understanding of what is happening there in order to counter it and in order to have an effective drugs strategy, which is what you are going to be part of being there to make sure happens.
Mr Howard: I think most of the profits go to enrich the key drugs traffickers. There is a range of people who have been identified as key players in this route. We will be very keen to help the Afghan authorities arrest these people and put them in jail. I do not want to go into details of that but that is personal enrichment. You ask the question whether there is any evidence that money from drug trafficking or narcotics in general is going to the Taliban. We have no evidence of any significant flow of money from narcotics traffickers to the Taliban or linkages in any other way. That is not to say that there might be some tactical contact between the two, but there is no evidence of that.

Q99 Linda Gilroy: We have been leading on this issue. There is the Afghan Drugs Interdepartmental Unit; there are 17 people in this country working on it and working closely, we understand, with a similar unit in the British Embassy. There must be some clear idea about what is happening. If we are actually going to be in there trying to bring stability, we have to counter that. What is the plan?
Mr Howard: Perhaps I can answer your point about the money and then go on to what the plan is that ADIDU, the Afghan Drugs Interdepartmental Unit, has set up. The point about the money is that the evidence we have so far shows that it is basically going to enrich criminals. That money is laundered through a number of means. I am not a law-enforcement expert and so I hope you will not press me too much on exactly how that happens. There are certainly people in ADIDU who would be able to give you that sort of information. That is the problem. In that sense, the problem of narcotics in Afghanistan is the same as the narcotics problem that exists elsewhere in the world; it essentially enriches criminals. That is what happens. I was trying to deal with the point I thought you were

making about the link to terrorism, which is why I said we have no evidence of a linkage there. In terms of how to deal with it, the Afghan Drugs Interdepartmental Unit has drawn up a comprehensive plan which covers a range of activities, all essentially in support of the Afghan Government. I am sorry to harp on about this but it is important that the Afghan Government is seen to be in the lead on this. One strand of that activity is interdiction; in other words, the arrest of high value and medium value targets associated with drugs. It would also include raids on laboratories and so on. The Afghan special narcotics force has been quite successful in that area. The counter-narcotics police also work in that area. The second strand is encouraging the establishment of an effective justice system. As I said, the Afghan Government has set up a special tribunal to deal with narcotics. The third is a programme of eradication, actually removing the crops on the ground. Very closely associated with that last one is of course the generation of alternative livelihoods for the farmers who grow it in the first place and who, at the moment, find themselves as kinds of prisoners of the trafficking system. Those are the four principal components of the plan. There is obviously lots of detail within that.

Chairman: I want to bring in Robert Key at this stage to ask about the detailed strategy.

Q100 Robert Key: Mr Howard, a lot of people ask what on earth are we doing in Afghanistan still and why are we going to send some more troops. The answer is clear, I think, and I support the Government wholeheartedly on this, that 95% of the heroin in this country comes from Afghanistan. It is a very serious problem the Government faces, and this is where it is caused. I believe that your responsibilities as Director General of Operational Policy also cover Latin America and the Caribbean?
Mr Howard: Yes, it does.

Q101 Robert Key: Can you therefore help us by explaining what is the difference in the approach to drug eradication for example in some of the Latin American countries compared to Afghanistan, because they are clearly very different, are they not?
Mr Howard: Yes. That is a slightly surprising question. I will try my best to answer it. If I do not satisfy your question on this occasion, I will let you have a note. First of all, it is a different drug. The key thing in the northern part of South America is cocaine as opposed to opium, so it is a different market. Secondly, what is mostly happening with the cocaine that is grown in the north of Latin America is that the majority ends up going to the United States. A chunk, but an important chunk nevertheless, comes to Europe. The way that it is being dealt with is in two parts and to which we make quite a small contribution. Primarily it is an American programme, as you will appreciate. The first programme is obviously inside the countries concerned: Colombia is the obvious example. It is to do with a very long-term programme of building government institutions. In some ways it is quite similar. Also, what did exist in Colombia but

perhaps less so now are whole no go areas controlled by the drug cartels. Part of the purpose of the Colombian authorities, supported by the US and others (and we have made a small contribution to that) has been to shrink those no go areas. That is one part of it. The second part of it is the actual interception of the movement of narcotics from the northern part of Latin America into the United States and, as I say, also into Europe. That has been an ongoing mission, which is an inter-agency mission; it is not just military. A lot of it is co-ordinated through a joint inter-agency task force based in Key West in Florida. There are many American agencies. We get involved in that.

Q102 Robert Key: Mr Howard, could I just short circuit this because of the point I am trying to make? In the Caribbean and Latin America it is civilian agencies which are primarily used, with some military assistance. Here it is the other way round: we are using the British Army primarily to try to crack this problem, but we are also up against a completely different factor. The Ministry of Defence memorandum to us tells us that the opium trade spreads into senior levels of government and controls some provincial administrations. We are now told today in a statement from the Foreign Office that the Bonn Agreement will be replaced by the Afghan Compact, which will last for another five years. This is going to be a very long-term project. Long after the International Security Assistance Force (ISAF) has withdrawn, this problem is going to carry on. Will ISAF withdraw in an orderly fashion or will it be expelled because the Governor of Afghanistan gets more confident and they do not want us there any more, particularly if you are dealing with such enormous levels of illiteracy in the police force: 90% of the 50,000 men working as police in Afghanistan, we are told, are untrained, poorly equipped and illiterate and owe their allegiance to local warlords and military commanders rather than central government. When will ISAF withdraw?
Mr Howard: I do not have a date when they will withdraw. The idea would be that they will withdraw when their task is complete. I would go back to the measures of effectiveness that I tried to set out at the beginning of this evidence session, recognising that some of them are subjective. I would also slightly question the assumption that this is primarily a military task. I think I did say explicitly earlier on that dealing with narcotics is not primarily a military task. It is important to promoting stability inside Afghanistan. To get to specifics, quite a lot of the components in the ADIDU plan, which I referred to, are not military. Forming the judicial system is not a military function. Building alternative livelihoods is not a military function. The military function is pretty well focused in fact, to my mind, on assisting the Afghan authorities in interdiction.

Q103 Robert Key: This is extremely risky and may get more risky for British forces. What is the level of risk which the British Government thinks is acceptable in terms of committing forces in an increasingly hostile region of Afghanistan? How many deaths is the Government prepared to take?

Mr Howard: I do not think we measure risk in those terms.

Q104 Robert Key: It will be the first time for some time that a government does not make those sorts of calculations.

Mr Howard: We do make calculations about the forces needed to carry out the task that we need to carry out as part of the NATO force. As part of our detailed planning, we will have made assumptions about casualty levels, but that is not the same as saying that we will only accept this many dead before we pull out. We do not really couch things in those terms.

Q105 Robert Key: What is the influence of Iran on all of this in terms of the penetration of information through the press, through television, the media? For example, what proportion of the Afghan population has television and radio receivers and listens to broadcasts?

Mr Howard: I do not have a detailed answer to that. What we find in Afghanistan is that the medium which is most used by ordinary citizens is in fact radio. If you want me to find out a bit more detail, I can do that.

Q106 Robert Key: PSY OPS[9] is clearly going to be very important in all of this, is it not?

Mr Howard: I think information operations in general it is going to be extremely important, yes.

Q107 Robert Key: Where are the opium growers expected to go if we chase them out? Will they go over the international boundaries and, if so, where will they go?

Mr Howard: Are you talking about the farmers?

Q108 Robert Key: Yes.

Mr Howard: I am not sure that it is very likely that the farmers would disappear and go and grow opium somewhere else. I think the important thing is that if we are successfully going to deal with the opium problem in Afghanistan, we need this multi-faceted approach. The two things most clearly to be co-ordinated are the process of eradication of opium crops and the availability of alternative livelihoods, and these are linked.

Q109 Robert Key: We do not believe in spraying them, do we? The Americans do but we do not.

Mr Howard: We do not believe that aerial eradication is the right answer and, perhaps more importantly, neither does President Karzai.

Q110 Robert Key: What are the current planning assumptions for the UK commitment and therefore withdrawal to ISAF? How long are we going to commit?

---

[9] *Note:* Psychological Operations.

Mr Howard: The Headquarters of ISAF is committed for nine months from May. That is pretty clear. We have not reached a final view on how long we would deploy British forces, but it will be for a set period. We do not intend to make it open-ended. I would see that when we decide and if we deploy substantial forces into the south of Afghanistan they would be there for a period. If you do not mind, I would rather not be drawn on what that period might be because I think the Secretary of State wants to say that. Then they would come out in an orderly fashion. This is the whole point, that we will come out in an orderly fashion. That would not mean necessarily that that would be the end of British military involvement inside Afghanistan. I could easily visualise that we would still be there involved in training and mentoring Afghan security forces as time goes on.

Q111 Linda Gilroy: My question is about narcotics and it is very brief. Just for the record, could you say which department leads on ADIDU and what the MoD contribution to it is?

Mr Howard: ADIDU is based in the Foreign Office and it is led by a Foreign Office diplomat. We provide a deputy from the MoD who is a military officer. I am afraid I do not have the exact numbers.

Q112 Linda Gilroy: Could you let us have a note on that?

Mr Howard: Yes, certainly, and I can cover funding as well.

Q113 Mr Hamilton: Could I briefly take you to two things you said and tie them together, if I can: firstly, narcotic problems are similar around the world; and, secondly, counter-narcotics is not primarily a military problem. Can I draw your attention to the very successful counter-narcotics organisation that was set up, in part, by the military police in Sarajevo in recent years and say that there have been some rumblings and concerns that because it is not primarily a military role, some of the lessons learnt from that organisation are not being taken forward to Afghanistan.

Mr Howard: I am not very familiar with the background to that particular unit. In looking at the Afghan problem, we have tried to look at the situation on the ground and what is needed. I am sorry to be rather tedious about this but a key player in this is the Afghan Government and this is about how we can support them to do that. I would stand by my point that if you want to deal with the totality of a narcotics problem, it is not primarily a military task. The military can help and support, but there needs to be the support of the civil authorities. There are two people from the MoD starting in ADIDU: the deputy and one team leader. We can give you a more detailed breakdown of the organisation, if you require that.

Q114 Chairman: I have one final question on narcotics. Alternative livelihoods I know is only one of the multi-faceted strands of approaches that you were talking about. In practice, how do you think it is possible to bring in alternative livelihoods to farmers who can earn 10 times the amount by growing opium?

Mr Howard: A number of things can be done. It is primarily a matter for my colleagues in DFID to develop the alternative livelihoods. In the past, Afghanistan has had a tradition of being quite successful growers of high value crops, and so on. That would be one of the alternatives. On the question of differentiation of profit, one answer to that is that if the traffickers are being caught and locked up and locked away, it makes it much more difficult for the farmer to get his money. That becomes a disincentive. Secondly, it is important to deal with the issue of debt which farmers have got into—debt to the traffickers in terms of buying seeds, which ties them in. There may be schemes whereby micro debt relief can be introduced. There is a range of things that can be done, including the availability of other forms of employment, which may not necessarily be farming. The experts here are in ADIDU and in DFID rather than me.

Chairman: We move on to the troops and assets.

Q115 Mr Havard: Can I bring you down to the basics of what is going to happen here, particularly with assets? I will not ask you the obvious question about whether you are confident we will send the right things, because I am sure you are. What I want to know is what you are actually going to send. There is a particular set of issues around rotary and fixed-wing aircraft that are required in Afghanistan. Could you say something about what is going to be deployed in order to achieve what is necessary with those parts of the component?

Mr Howard: It is a bit difficult for me to be precise, Mr Havard, because, as I say, the Secretary of State has not reached a final view, and he will want to announce it. As I said, I think there will be an aviation package as part of this. Having helicopters there will be an important element of both mobility and force protection. If you are asking me to give you numbers, I do not think I can do that.

Q116 Mr Havard: Never mind the numbers. Let us look at the general concept of it. The C-17s are playing a huge role in terms of getting people to and from the country. They are also playing a role within the country, which probably was not quite envisaged originally in the way that is happening at moment. We have Hercules and various helicopters. The problem with lift is a particular set of issues within that country and it is going to become more important. If we are going to use the Afghan National Army as a set of assets, for example, they do not have any capacity to manoeuvre without the allies, ISAF, actually giving them that capacity. We are going to be moving them as well as moving our own. This whole question about lift in terms of helicopters and fixed-wing aircraft is of huge importance. What is being done in order to revise that strategy because you need a hell of a lot more than you currently have?

Mr Howard: It is certainly important. Chris will speak about where we are in relation to this in general.

Air Vice Marshal Chris Nickols: I would disagree with that final statement that we need a lot more than we currently have. We will only put a force package in that can be supported with the lift that we have and that it needs, more to the point. It will be, as you say, a combination of C-130s for the distance and the heavy lift and helicopters. Of course, helicopters are not the only way to move around. Much of what the forces need to do has to be done on the ground out there patrolling, providing a secure environment and such like. It is not all helicopter movement. We would not put a force package in that was not balanced, as we call it; in other words, one that did not have the helicopters that we felt it needed to do its job properly and safely.

Mr Havard: I can advance you an argument, having been there and stood on various bits of tarmac and sand. Airplanes have had to be re-tasked; they could not go where they wanted to go and they had to go later. There is an issue about the amount of support that there is. We will leave that for another day. What about the other air component then?

Q117 Chairman: Before we do that, Air Vice Marshal Ian McNichol said that he could not maintain the airlift into Iraq last week, as I understand it. Is that right?

Air Vice Marshal Chris Nickols: I am not sure that he put it precisely in those terms. There were some problems with the latest movement of troops into Iraq. In essence, some of the aircraft hit a bad period of serviceability and there were some delays putting some people in. I think that was what he was talking about. As it happens, various measures have been taken, particularly on spares re-supply, that have got over that problem and the serviceability has much improved at the moment.

Q118 Chairman: If we cannot maintain the deployment we have in Iraq, when we expand into Afghanistan, what confidence can we have that we will be able to maintain the deployment there?

Air Vice Marshal Chris Nickols: The particular issue was on a change-over of troops, and so what we would call a surge period for air transport rather than routine maintenance and sustainment of the operations. It was not a problem in routine terms.

Q119 Mr Hancock: We knew six months ago that they were rotating in that period of time, that the troops were comign in and out of the country. The RAF did not know, obviously.

Air Vice Marshal Chris Nickols: No, it was that several airplanes, and of course—

Q120 Mr Hancock: They were out of service at the same time?

Air Vice Marshal Chris Nickols: You have to bear in mind that the aircraft we are talking about are Tri-Star aircraft that, for instance, carry 250 to 300 people, and so if one of them does become unserviceable or, say, a couple become unserviceable, the spare one you had, then you do end up with quite a large quantity of people waiting while you fix the aircraft before you can then move them. The stress on the air transport fleet that he was talking about was caused by the surge of change-over of troops, which of course in Iraq is nearly 8,000 troops.

Chairman: Can I repeat something that Dai Havard has said? We will need to come back to this because the Ministry of Defence has tried to be reassuring about lift. I think this Committee is far from reassured.

Q121 Mr Havard: That is right. I am chasing the clock here, so I was cutting down my questions. There are a lot more questions I could have asked you about this. Other people are going to deploy assets, I know, so it is not just British assets that will be in there. There is the whole question about the appropriateness of certain asssets that are going in as well, some of which seem to be more related to pork-barrel politics in America than they do about anything else, but we will come back to all of that another day. The jets, the Harriers, the combat support, is particularly important, not just simply for British troops but for the whole of the ISAF operation and the counter-terrorism operation. Currently we have the GR7s in Kandahar. The runway is not finished. It is taking longer that the Great Wall of China, it seems, in order to complete. As I understand it, the Harriers are due to come out in the summer. This is where we have to ask you a few questions about the Dutch. When I was in Kabul, the F16s are in Kabul flying about; the Dutch have 16 of those. As I understand it, if Dutch troops come, they have to bring their own combat air support, and that is the F16s. The F16s are designed to replace the Harriers to give overall air combat support, as I understand it. What is going to be deployed? We have the Harriers there for the initial period when the troops go in. What is going to be the sustainability of combat air support—full stop?

Air Vice Marshal Chris Nickols: The simple answer is that fixed-wing air support is subject to the same force of generation process as any other asset that is going in. Clearly, not every nation takes in its own fixed-wing air support. As I have already said earlier, in broad terms, fixed-wing air support is pretty inter-operable. The Harrier GR7s at the moment are in Afghanistan, as you say, until the summer—mid-summer I think it is—of 2006, but no decisions have been finalised on the NATO force generation process and what air support will be available beyond that. I would clearly say, of course, that nationally we have to be absolutely sure that our troops on the ground must receive the air support that they might need before we will be happy to put them in there on the ground. If you like, it is just another asset and we need to be absolutely sure that we get the support that we need, whether that be UK aircraft or other aircraft.

Q122 Mr Havard: The answer at the moment is that

you are reassured by that because the Harriers are there for the initial period, but we do not know that that is going to provide support in the longer term.
Air Vice Marshal Chris Nickols: Of course, it is not always Harriers that provide air support. It could be American aircraft or whatever. There are not just UK aircraft in Afghanistan at the moment.

Q123 Mr Havard: So my sly fiver on a few Tornadoes going out there later in the year might come to fruition yet then? That was not a question. What assurances have you had because you make the point, and you are quite right, that it is not just the British who give close air support? The big aviation assets in the country are obviously those of the US. What discussions have you had with the US about some continued support, as it were, given that they are changing their formation of operations there? Operation Enduring Freedom is going to end; that is not an oxymoron but it is going to transform into something else; they are going to downsize to some degree or another. In those sorts of circumstances, what discussions have you had with the US that there will be continuing levels of support during that period and in through the rest of the period that the ARC is there through into 2007?
Air Vice Marshal Chris Nickols: The simple answer is that we have to work through NATO because it is a NATO plan and US forces will be assigned to NATO, just as UK forces or any other nations' forces will be. The US will fill quite a large proportion of the air requirement in that NATO force generation process.

Q124 Mr Hamilton: You have indicated that credibility is on the line on NATO. You have also indicated that there are 50,000 police with a justice system that has been developed by the Italians, which I find quite interesting. You have 28,000 in the Army in Afghanistan. You have an increase in suicide bombers. Pakistan has a problem, particularly as far as bombers are concerned. The Dutch, and maybe some other nations, have to decide in relation to whether they come in or not. We have warlords which are governors in some cases and governors who are warlords in other cases. We have the Taliban resurgence. I am asking you a specific question, not about any of those factors but about our own armed forces, so maybe we can get a straight answer in relation to that. A lot of the things that we are talking about in relation to Afghanistan are predicated on whether we are able to reduce our armed forces in Iraq. If that does not take place, are we going to be a position of being over-stretched, recognising that we are going into a far more dangerous position than British troops have already been in? My question to you is quite clear but straightforward. If things do not work out the way that we hope they will work out in other places and we can release British troops and British forces, are we in a position to take up the slack in relation to Afghanistan?
Mr Howard: In broad terms, yes, we can. Chris can talk about some of the detail if you like. This is a question we ask ourselves all the time. We are

making planning assumptions about how things might go in Iraq and how things might go in Afghanistan. Like all plans, they may vary on contact with reality. Throughout the process, the Secretary of State rightly asks the same question. We have given him the assurance that we can do both. That is not to say we can do both completely easily. There will be areas of pressure as a result. The areas are likely to be less in terms of strengths of infantry battalions or anything like that but more in terms of the key enabling tasks. The two that immediately occur to me will be medical support and intelligence support, and so we will have to manage those difficulties. The broad answer to your question is: yes, we can manage both.

Q125 Mr Lancaster: In order to achieve both, what sacrifices will you have to make to the Harmony Guidelines on back-to-back tours?
Mr Howard: It is difficult to give an absolutely precise answer to that because there are so many variables about that.

Q126 Mr Lancaster: Will there be any sacrifices?
Mr Howard: I think that in certain key trades there will be issues of pressure and issues on Harmony. I have mentioned a couple of examples and there could be others. These are not things which would prevent the deployment taking place. It is a fact that

the British Armed Forces have been very busy for some years and that there are areas where Harmony Guidelines have been breached. The Chiefs of Staff take a very close interest in that and they charge a Deputy Chief of Defence Staff (Personnel) to take measures to alleviate that. It is hard to say that this trade will suffer this change because it will depend on, (a), what happens in Iraq, and, (b), the precise nature of what we deploy into Afghanistan. The point at which, for example, we take over leadership of the brigade in the south of Afghanistan is a variable which has not yet been nailed down.

Q127 Chairman: Which trade is most at risk of having its Harmony Guidelines breached?
Mr Howard: Can I come back to you with a precise answer on that? I do not think I could say definitely one way or the other. Medical staff will probably be high on my list but we will come back and give you a precise answer.
Chairman: There are one or two questions which we would like to have asked you about provincial reconstruction teams but, in view of the time, it would be best to write to you about those, if that is all right. Unless anyone has any further questions arising out of this, then I would simply say thank you very much indeed, both of you, for coming along this morning and for answering the questions to the extent that is permissible and to which you are able.

Tuesday 7 March 2006

Members present:

Mr James Arbuthnot, in the Chair

Mr David S Borrow	Mr Adam Holloway
Linda Gilroy	Mr Brian Jenkins
Mr David Hamilton	Robert Key
Mr Mike Hancock	Mr Mark Lancaster
Mr Dai Havard	John Smith

Witnesses: **Rt Hon Adam Ingram,** a Member of the House, Minister of State for the Armed Forces, **Air Marshal Sir Glenn Torpy KCB CBE,** Commander of Joint Operations PJHQ, and **Dr Roger Hutton,** Director Joint Commitments Policy, Ministry of Defence, and **Mr Peter Holland,** Head of the Afghan Drugs Inter-Departmental Unit (ADIDU), Foreign and Commonwealth Office, gave evidence.

Q128 Chairman: Minister, good morning and welcome to this evidence session on Afghanistan. I wonder whether it might be helpful first for us to say that we know you have to leave at 12.00 and we will not be clinging on to everyone else once you have left but we will bring the whole evidence session to an end in time for you to leave then. Minister, I wonder whether you could possibly introduce your team, who are all very welcome.

Mr Ingram: I am grateful for that co-operation. As you appreciate, I have got an adjournment debate on another subject and that is the reason for my departure. I would be only too happy, of course, to stay here all day to get to the conclusion of your inquiry. In fact, I would even be able to assist you in writing a report if you wanted that! Obviously we recognise the importance of this subject and that is why I have what we would call a very heavyweight team with me today because they are the subject experts. On my right is Air Marshal Sir Glenn Torpy, who is CJO. On his right is Dr Roger Hutton, who is Director Joint Commitments Policy, and on my left is Peter Holland who heads up the Afghan Drugs Inter-Departmental Unit. I understand that you may want to explore some of the subject matter on the counter-narcotics side of it. We are now here to assist as best we can.

Q129 Chairman: Thank you very much. When the deployment was agreed a year ago things in Afghanistan looked rather better than they do now. How would you describe the situation in relation to the security situation in Afghanistan at the moment?

Mr Ingram: I will answer your question specifically but you are right in saying when we looked at this initially that there was a different climate than that which exists now. It would seem to me that, no matter what the climate was, the imperative of us as part of an international force helping the Afghan Government to deal with that emerging country and the way in which it is developing would have continued nonetheless, but clearly circumstances which prevail on the ground then have to be taken into account in terms of force generation and in terms of other aspects. If anything, the climate overall could be defined as being much better, but we will deal with the threat level separately from that because now we have a better and well-established

government, a better-focused government, one that has a large measure of very tangible buy-in from the international community as substance rather than words—and the London Conference was a very clear example of all of that—so the overall governance of Afghanistan is unquestionably better than it was a year ago, and all credit to President Karzai and those who work closely with him to help to deliver all of that. I think that is one parameter which in many ways makes our mission and our objectives easier to obtain because it is not Iraq, let us describe it that way. There are many more beneficial indicators in there, ie they have a government, they have been through that process, and probably in the overall commitment of the international community it has a better view of what is happening in Afghanistan than what is happening in Iraq. Some people try to compare them and I make this point; they are not comparable; no two areas of involvement are. In the Balkans, Bosnia is different from Kosovo. On the specifics on the threat level happening on the ground, I think it can be over-stated. There is no question at all that there have been some pretty serious incidents and tragically lives have been lost as a consequence of all of that. It would seem to me that that was always going to be the case, that the closer we got to focusing on the ground as we developed our presence in co-operation with the Afghan Government from the north and the west as we moved towards the south, that that was always going to stimulate that type of reaction from those who are hostile to us. While there are indicators of a Taliban presence on the ground, it is not an overwhelming presence, and it is not what it was. There is a threat level there. There are certainly risks involved in what we are going to be doing there and there are also indications that al-Qaeda will be looking at this as well, remembering that al-Qaeda is very much the focus, indeed terrorism is very much the focus of Operation Enduring Freedom. You will have witnessed the discussions which have taken place between President Karzai and President Musharraf and between President Bush and President Musharraf to try and ensure that we have that concerted pressure in the border regions, which we will not principally be involved in. Much progress has been made but, as ever, those who want to put pressure on us will continue to do the things which they are capable of doing. What we cannot do is allow them to succeed, and nor will we.

Q130 Chairman: Who is responsible for the upsurge in violence? Would you say that it was al-Qaeda, the Taliban, warlords, or would you equate all three or only two of those?

Mr Ingram: As someone said to me, sometimes it depends on when they get up in the morning they will put on a particular uniform. It depends who is paying them and so, as ever, our intelligence can never be 100% perfect in all of this and it is a mixture of all of those. With increasing focus on and increasing success in the counter-narcotics area, we are taking the senior players out and there is the interdiction activity that goes on. However, given the nature of those who want to participate in such trade (which is very valuable to them so they may well be paying people to do things) they are prepared to do it themselves anyway, so it is a mixture, but the potency of it and the scale of it should not be over-reacted to in the sense that it can be managed and it will be managed in other ways, ie that is what the PRTs are for, that is what the central government approach is in terms of what President Karzai is trying to achieve, and it is managing the wider community so that those who may be purchasable, who may be committed to doing something can find an alternative for them not to do so. It is taking away that ground support, and that will not happen overnight.

Q131 Chairman: You are being very reassuring, Minister, but perhaps overly so. Some of the violence that was quelled recently was quelled by ISAF troops. What is the capacity of the Afghanistan security forces?

Mr Ingram: I do not want to sound reassuring or indeed complacent because the language we use—and I will restate that—is that this is not a risk-free environment and we do anticipate—and I made this point and I will make it again—that there will be attacks on us. In terms of the formation of that threat and where it comes from, we are still best understanding it, and clearly in times past and in recent times past they have been prepared to stand up in numbers, which has resulted in sometimes OEF forces and sometimes ISAF forces taking that on and also, importantly, Afghan forces taking them on, usually in concert with each other. Where there is a sizable presence, where they do stand up, then they now well understand the potency of our reaction. If I have to guess anything it will mean that they change their *modus operandi.* We have no complacency in there and we have certainly no reassurance that they have gone away. In fact they will be there. They are capable, intelligent people and they will continue to pose a very real threat to us. In terms of the Afghan capabilities, of course they have been growing measurably. There are a very significant number of Afghan trained and equipped personnel—I think the figure is in the region of 34,000—and a significant number of

trained police officers as well. In terms of what will happen in the south, already 1,000 Afghan troops have been committed, with more to follow, and clearly in terms of the training of those troops the intention is to get the capabilities up to make sure that they turn up on the day. That always remains an issue that has to be addressed. However, I have a lot of confidence in General Wardak whom I have met on a number of occasions and who is the Afghan Defence Minister. He is a very experienced military commander in his own right. He will know where the quality is and what can be done, and he will also know where improvements need to be made. So he is a driver for change as well in all of this and that works its way right through the Afghan senior administration.

Q132 Chairman: Colonel Worsley said to *The Guardian*: "They are our exit strategy—a well trained, well led Afghan Army", but we are nowhere close to that yet, are we?

Mr Ingram: No, we are not and in a sense the exit strategy in any area where there has been conflict is building the capacity of the host nation. That applies in the Balkans, that applies in Iraq, and it is clearly going to apply in Afghanistan. As we have indicated before, and I think it is the iron law of such situations, the civil police are usually the last to get full competency and yet they become the key ingredient because that is the key indicator of normalcy beginning to apply. That does take time. So we are not there yet but it is not by failure on the part of the international community to lift that capacity—and I know that is not the point that you are making—nor is it a lack of willingness on the part of the Afghan Government. I mention General Wardak again. Increasingly amongst the Afghan people they themselves are willing to engage. They want a different society. There is not an off-the-shelf solution that says do all these things and you will automatically get it the day after tomorrow. It does not work that way. There will be many points along the road where we have to deal with those issues and maybe because of what is happening in the counter-narcotics sector it is creating a reaction within the community, and that is why we have to grow all of that capacity in terms of alternative livelihoods and, to use the word again, to create a condition of normalcy that people have confidence that if they go down our route and the route preferred by their own Government and that which they have voted for, then that will continue to grow, and the capacity of the country to deliver for them will continue to grow. It will not happen overnight, even with the massive resources being put in both in people and in projects through alternative livelihoods and so on.

Q133 Chairman: Mr Holland, I do not know whether you wanted to come in there. We will be coming on to the issue of narcotics towards the end. I do not know whether you have anything you want to add immediately to that very briefly?

Mr Holland: I know that you will be talking about it, as you say, in a bit more detail at the end, but I think that is absolutely right that in terms of the counter-narcotics programme it must fit as part of the whole wider reconstruction and stabilisation effort. It is part of that whole effort to build Afghan government capacity and Afghan institutions. As part of that we are also trying to build specific counter-narcotics institutions, so a specific counter-narcotics police force, a specific part of the justice system to try narcotics criminals within so there are specific activities on the counter-narcotics side as well as that wider institutional development.

Q134 Mr Havard: Am I right in what you are saying then, which is that essentially for none or one of these groups, either in combination or singularly, the assessment has not changed that they do not present a strategic threat, however they do possess potency in certain places at certain times, so the uncertainty is uneven as opposed to it being a strategic problem. Is that essentially the same because that is what I understand it to have been previously?

Mr Ingram: What I do not want to do is to minimise the threat in all of this because the way in which they can attack, they have shown, they can be very specific in what they do and they can bring imported new technology into it as well, and we have to monitor all of that. These are the most difficult forms of attack to compete against in many ways, but we recognise that is the sort of threat that is out there. However, to use the Iraq analogy, there is not that measurable level of insurgency, there is not a campaign at present but, who knows, there are, again, no certainties and no-one has got the wisdom to say with 100% certainty how things will develop, but there is no evidence of subdivision or disaggregation of the communities such as in the form of important forces in large numbers. The ground conditions in terms of creating the right climate for that to happen have been well examined and well looked at, and in a sense has been significantly achieved both in the north and the west with the PRTs that are there. Mazar-e-Sharif is a good example of where we have contributed. In the early days of that there were trouble points which we had to deal with and had to quell. It never manifested itself into anything really substantial and I would expect those very same spikes to happen. We have to plan for all of those spikes to happen.

Q135 Mr Havard: Given this question about what the Afghan capability is, we are talking about the Afghan National Army and its capability, but the point was made just now really about the police. There is the counter-narcotics police force, there is a special narcotics force and so on. There is a sort of *carabinieri*-type activity to them. The last time I went there and saw the Afghan National Army they were very capable as individuals, and trained up to be so, but the question about how well they are equipped and how well they are able to manoeuvre and co-ordinate between one another, however, is a

different question. I understand it is a question of development but is that developing to such an extent that it is becoming more capable and how much more capable?

Mr Ingram: I will ask the CJO to come in in a moment but the answer to that is that they are improving their capabilities all the time. They are not a modern army, they are not a modern fighting force, they do not have all the resources that we will have but they will have that in support of them. Increasingly, General Wardak is looking at how best to grow those capabilities. The debate obviously has to be within the Afghan Government. They have got to decide their priorities and what they are going to do, but there is a growing competency there. It will increase over time. The more success we have, the more we are able to measure that and to say here is what has effectively been delivered, the confidence will grow and therefore the more capable both the commanders and the troops on the ground will become. This must be an iterative, developing process. This is not something you can simply deliver in one big tranche no matter what the activity is. The CJO may wish to comment on that.

Air Marshal Sir Glenn Torpy: I think the Minister's comment that the environment in the south is going to be less benign than the north is something which the Committee accepts. That is no surprise. The security architectures down in the south are less well developed than in the north. It is the heartland of the Taliban and we obviously have porous borders. So we accept that the environment is not going to be as easy as in the north and we have configured our force robustly to be able to cater for the threat that we see. In terms of the Afghan National Army and the Afghan National Police, the aim is to train approximately 70,000 in the Afghan National Army. That is the US's responsibility as the G8 lead and at the moment we have trained about 27,000 and in the country at the moment they amount to about 34,000. Of course, that is one of the main tasks that the UK force will be doing down in Helmand. It will be continuing the training that the Americans have started with the ANA. We will continue that by partnering and embedding our training teams with the ANA brigade which is earmarked to arrive in Helmand Province progressively over the course of the next 18 months. On the police side, the police are meant to be some 64,000 strong and at the moment between the Germans (who are the G8 lead for police training) and the Americans, they have trained about 46,000. So there is a gradual increase in capacity which we have accepted. This is exactly what we are doing in Iraq with the Iraqi-security forces and whilst we are building their capacity we are providing the secure environment so that reconstruction and redevelopment can occur at the same time and working very much along the same principles as we have seen in Iraq.

Q136 Mr Jenkins: I do not want to go over the same ground, Minister, but I am still lacking a feel for it, to be honest. I do not want to put words into your mouth—I never would—but since we are comparing it with a capable army to take over and run Afghanistan, on a scale of naught to ten, given all the considerations we have got (and I am not talking about the total force number I am talking about its capability its effectiveness) where would you put it? Would you put it at three or above? If we have got an exit strategy, do we expect to hand a province over to the Afghans to see if they can actually contain it and run it as it rolls out as a protective national force which should be effectively controlling this country?

Mr Ingram: I do not think we measure forces in scales of nought to 10. I have nothing more to add. I am sorry I cannot reassure you on this and nor can the CJO reassure you on this. This is a very significant number of people who are trained and equipped for the tasks they will be asked to do. I have indicated there are problems with that. I have indicated that will increase over time on the basis of success, and I think there is too much talk about exit strategies because what does that mean? Does that mean that there will be then no presence at all in terms of the international presence? Does it mean there will be some? Does it mean on a scale of nought to 10 something else? I think people have got hung up on this exit strategy. The strategy is to create the conditions where, effectively, we allow for good governance to take place, which is what the Afghans want and what the Afghan administration is seeking to achieve, and the security environment is absolutely fundamental to all of that. Who knows what the counter-terrorist activity may require in the years ahead. Will we still be there? We have got to make sure and well understand why we are there. We do not want—and it is enlightened self-interest— that threat that came and attacked New York and Washington and Pennsylvania, the terrible events that occurred in September those years ago, and we do not want the conditions to apply again. However, we are up against a range of attitudes and people who are not going to go away. They are determined to do what they are going to do so we have got to stop the conditions to allow them to foster and to grow. To give some definition of when that is going to happen timewise, I think is just simply not possible. However, the scale and the pace of change, if we get all of the things right that we are seeking to do, will be very marked and very noticeable and the buy-in will be very significant from the Afghan people themselves who, ultimately, will be the key ingredient in all of this. Government has a big part to play, the security presence on the ground can have a big part to play, but if there is no buy-in from the people themselves then it becomes much more difficult and therefore long-lasting. That is why all we are seeking to do is to achieve that at the ground level.

Dr Hutton: If I may just add something on the issue about the Afghan National Army. Where they have shortcomings at the moment is in terms of their logistics and self-sustainability, and some of their technical ability, for example calling in close air support, but what I would say is that the experience of British soldiers who have operated in close proximity to them in the north is that their tactics and procedures are progressing well. We have been very pleasantly surprised with how capable they have been. So the basic quality of the Afghan soldier is good. It is filling in all those gaps to make them self-sustaining in due course.

Q137 Mr Borrow: Minister, I want to pursue the point you made about the reason we are there in the first place. The Secretary of State has said that we have got a strong national interest in being involved in Afghanistan. I sometimes wonder what do I say to constituents as to why seven years after the Taliban regime fell we have still got troops there who have been put in harm's way. You seem to be saying that the reason that we are still there, the reason we are still involved is the feeling that if we were not the Taliban regime would come to power again and provide a haven for al-Qaeda. Is that the strategic reason that the UK has got involvement there rather than any other reason? Is that the key national interest?

Mr Ingram: We have a national and an international interest in all this because remembering it was the US that was attacked, and if we removed ourselves and it became a wholly ungovernable space again, it does not necessarily mean that the Taliban come back into power, but if it is an ungovernable space the bad elements can fill that vacuum and they can use it for training grounds and they can use it for a whole lot of other purposes. They can even use the narcotics trade and the large volumes of money that come from all of that to assist them in all of this. They are not going to do it for benign reasons. It is not because they want self-government. It is not because they want to be left alone. It is because they want to grow that capability to attack us. So the international community well understands this, as does President Karzai and his senior people, and increasingly there is a significant buy-in from the Afghan people. They do not want to be known as the pariahs of the international community. The road to renewal is unquestionably going to be difficult but we cannot allow it to go back to anything like it was or anything approximating to it because the threat to us is very significant. That does not even deal with the narcotics issue which is out there as well and, as we know, 90% of what they produce there ends up on the streets of our country. So we have another area of interest in trying to deal with that as well because of the death and desolation that can bring to so many families and indeed micro communities within the UK.

Q138 Mr Borrow: You will be aware of the argument that has been made by many people that if you looked at the history of Afghanistan there has very rarely been a strong central state, that it has never been a country with a strong government apart from very short periods, usually periods that we would welcome the return of. So there is an argument that the task of trying to bring about a stable, democratic government in Afghanistan may not be worth the effort and in that perspective could I just bring you back—

Mr Ingram: Sorry, worth the effort to whom?

Q139 Mr Borrow: Worth the effort to the international community in that we have got troops and we have got all of the effort that has been put in to reconstruct. Looking specifically at the work of ISAF in Afghanistan, what would you say was a realistic aim and objective over the next three years for them to achieve in Afghanistan because obviously we ought to be having some sort of target as to what our effort and expenditure and everything else will achieve while they are there? What would you say was realistic over the next three years to be achieved?

Mr Ingram: I think all the ingredients we have set out to achieve, and perhaps are best articulated and discussed in commitments arising from those discussions at the London Conference, are about creating that freedom for the Afghan people to determine their own future, to give them the security, working alongside them, to achieve all of that, to create the conditions where people have the buy-in to a normal type of society. It is not our type of society but what they would expect and want, and that would be the right to look after their families, to have some economic future, hopefully to move large numbers of them away from subsistence farming, and to give them the prospect of economic growth in the future. Remembering there was a time when Afghanistan was a major exporter, I am not an expert in this area but it was at one time a fairly successful economy. That does not mean to say there were not large areas of poverty—undoubtedly there were—but all of that was knocked off course because of the events of decades past. In terms of have they ever had central government: in many ways the United Kingdom at one time did not have strong central government but we grew it and now over recent time it has improved, and is a capable central government over even more recent times. The point is: do the people of Afghanistan want that? That is a matter for them so to decide. We cannot impose that. However, there are very clear indicators, and with the elections that took place and the way in which people committed themselves to those elections, they realise there is a better future; they want to part of it but cannot deliver it on their own. That is what the international community is seeking to achieve. If we create those conditions and it does develop in that way it then does not represent an area, a territory of one governable space, into which those evil elements would be able to grow. I cannot speak for the Afghan people, only they can speak for themselves in this, but they do not want those people on their doorstep. They do not want them doing what they are doing, and that is what they have indicated in terms of what they are seeking to achieve. Whether it means a completely, wholly united country—let them develop that themselves. We have only in recent decades got into devolution in this country. We have gone from one construct and we are evolving still, both as an economy and as a governed entity. I will not go into a debate on devolution right now.

Q140 Mr Borrow: You mentioned earlier, Minister, that you were reluctant to deal with an exit strategy; and I accept from where we are now it is difficult to set a date for the withdrawal of troops etc; but are you actually saying to the Committee you anticipate international involvement, including UK involvement, in Afghanistan for a long period of time in the future?

Mr Ingram: We are committed to the three years' commitment. There are 36 nations currently engaged. This can only be measured as a policy in the future, but as we begin to achieve success the mission will change anyway once the ISAF Stage 3 mission in the south does deliver (and I have every confidence it will because of the capabilities put there); and the direction in which it will move will create conditions and therefore Stage 4 then comes into the ambit of ISAF. I have given an indication there will probably still be a threat out there from terrorist elements that will have to be dealt with and that again is at some point in the future. When people talk about an "exit strategy", I think the entrance strategy defines the exit and that is what we are doing. That is why we have spent so long defining what it is we are seeking to achieve in the south, which is less benign, which has a lot of elements that have to be dealt with. If we can achieve that (and I am very positive that can be achieved) then that creates a flavour of success. It will be foolhardy to say, "At the end of three years it's over"; I think that would be wrong; or, "At the end of five years it's over". We do not know this will develop. All the indicators are of improvements that could suddenly become very rapid and then we would have to consider: why are we there; what more should we be doing; what less should we be doing, what the balance of all of this is; where is the threat; how we are achieving success in terms of counter-narcotics; and what other elements are out there that still have to be addressed? It is too futuristic to give definitions now.

Q141 Mr Hancock: If I could ask two quick questions. One is about the quality of intelligence. You said rightly, Minister, that some of the groups in Afghanistan decide in the morning when they get up which side they are going to be on. What does that do for our forces there and who they have to work with; and how good is the quality and nature of the intelligence we are working to? Secondly, when the Secretary General of the UN was in this room speaking he said that the biggest mistake in Afghanistan was not disarming the warlords. Do you really believe it is possible for an Afghan military force to have countrywide quality control of the country while there are so many armed groups who are significantly opposed to the central government and, unless they are removed in one way or another, the situation will be that an under-resourced army will never be able to compete with that situation?

Mr Ingram: I do not take your last point of an "under-resourced army" if you mean the force we are putting in.

Q142 Mr Hancock: No, not our army, the Afghan Army. You said, Minister, that there was a lack of resources for the Afghan Army and that was part of the failure at the present time?

Mr Ingram: It is part of the issue which has to be addressed. This failure at the present time, remember we are only a short number of years away from the end of the removal of the Taliban regime and for them to grow a modern army with all the attributes in that timescale is just not realistic and anyone who made such a demand would be living in a fantasy world, to think that someone could so produce it. The question of intelligence on the ground and the way in which the threat can reshape and refocus, that is what we seek best to do, to best understand that. It is what much of the activity of the PRT will be able to do, about getting buy-in from what wider community. There are a whole lot of things we will go into to encourage all of that, and engagement of the people to give us information so we have a better understanding and, indeed, that will mean talking to some of those people who are posing the threat. It is no different from any other approach we have had to adopt from Northern Ireland onwards, and perhaps even before Northern Ireland. You have to understand what is causing the problem; you have to see what measure you can put in place to mitigate that and deal with it; and to create the conditions so that does not continue to grow and manifest itself. It has taken us 30 years in Northern Ireland, which one would have thought was a much easier equation; but I do not want that to be used as an indicator that it is 30 years' commitment to Afghanistan, but I point out the problems. I think our knowledge now of dealing with all of this is so much better, by and large because we do not have the great standoffs that applied at the time of the Cold War and all the geopolitical manoeuvring that went on which allowed a lot of unrest to foster for other purposes. Those conditions do not really apply globally now the way they once did. There is a much clearer international focus to try and resolve these problems because everyone is at threat from that—everyone; because the minute they topple one part of the temple they will come for the next bit.

Chairman: We are falling behind. Could I ask for both short questions and for shorter answers please, Minister.

Q143 Mr Holloway: Notwithstanding the huge damage done by heroin in this country, are we not slightly confusing our aims? If we want to have stability in Afghanistan and also reduce the quantity of drugs coming into this and other countries, how can you do that? How can you get buy-in from the Afghan people if you are assisting the ANA in destroying their livelihoods?

Mr Holland: The first point is that the vast majority of Afghan people actually are not involved in the drugs trade themselves—it is only about eight or 9% of the population who are directly involved in the trade. All the surveys which have been carried out do indicate that, there again, the majority of the population would like to see the back of the drugs trade. That said clearly there is a risk where you are tackling the trade, and particularly eradicating crops, that that does have a response. Eradication of crops is only one element of a much wider strategy in terms of tackling the drugs trade, and that encompasses building government institutions, building law enforcement capacity, the justice system as well as putting in place alternative livelihoods and development in those areas.

Chairman: We will come onto this in much greater detail. I keep saying this but we will, I promise. Can I move on to John Smith and NATO?

Q144 John Smith: NATO and the Stage 3 expansion. Minister, the delays experienced in the NATO force generation process, do you think that reveals a reluctance or an unwillingness on some contributor nations to get involved in the more dangerous work in the less benign south of Afghanistan?

Mr Ingram: I suppose every contributing nation, ourselves included, has to examine what it is they are seeking to do. Do we have the capability to do it? What is the public mood? Winning that public mood in some countries may be more difficult than here. It may even become difficult here in relation to what David Borrow asked about how you justify it. That is where I think we all have an obligation to play in this—to make sure that, hopefully, the way in which I have articulated it, the way in which the Secretary of State has and, even more so, the Prime Minister, as to the vitality of what we are seeking to do and the absolute importance of what we are seeking, encourages our own people in the UK, but also internationally as well. I do not think we need to convince the United States—being the victim of what happened I think they are very focussed and targeted—but there will still be noises off in the United States about it, but it is about the steely determination of government to define what the mission is and then do we have the capability? I think in many ways the way in which we have gone about it shows that we have not just jumped at the problem and I have participated in most of the discussions, if not all of the discussions, as this has begun to be put in place. It has been carefully analysed and there is not a military solution alone; there is no point just putting a military force into the country and expecting it all to be resolved; we have to have all of those other ingredients in place. The London conference was a good example and I am sure that encouraged other contributing nations to see the strength of the case; and that will then encourage both parliaments and, hopefully, the people to understand the importance of it. Will it go up and down? Yes, it will. It is the very nature of this, but the NATO force generation has unquestionably put in place a very importance force; and those who are preparing to resist it should well understand that. This is a powerful force that has been put in place here which will deliver on that mission and will create the conditions to let other things grow.

7 March 2006   Rt Hon Adam Ingram MP, Air Marshal Sir Glenn Torpy KCB CBE, Dr Roger Hutton and Mr Peter Holland

Q145 John Smith: Good. I think the answer was, yes!
Mr Ingram: I did not know you wanted that short an answer!
Chairman: We do want short answers!

Q146 John Smith: A good answer nonetheless! Are we confident that ISAF rules of engagement are sufficiently robust to help us tackle the challenges in the south? Is there any concern about national caveats undermining the consistency of response to insurgents across Afghanistan?
Mr Ingram: Yes, to the first part. We will have to see what caveats prevail, if any do prevail, and to encourage those (if they were coming in and putting caveats that were just making everybody else's job more difficult) not to do so. I think we have learnt considerably from some of those problems in the Balkans where the national caveats really were a constraint. People who are committing want to achieve the mission. I do not think they are there just for the tokenism of it.

Q147 John Smith: On the rules of engagement and the remit to protect and deter, will that allow our forces to take offensive action against forces that are threatening ours and pursue and destroy such forces if they attack us and then flee?
Mr Ingram: I think the answer to that is, yes, but we never discuss rules of engagement. I think it is wrong to explore it in any great detail. I think the way in which I have understood the question if you want a quick answer, then the answer to that would be, yes.

Q148 John Smith: You are satisfied?
Mr Ingram: We would not be doing it if we were not satisfied.
Air Marshal Sir Glenn Torpy: If I could reinforce the Minister's point. From a military perspective, and that is clearly where I focus in the PJHQ, we are content that the rules of engagement that are now contained in the NATO OPLAN are sufficient to match the tasks that we are going to be asked to do.

Q149 John Smith: Good. Are we prepared to reinforce UK troops if the numbers that we deploy prove to be insufficient?
Mr Ingram: We have said that we have to measure what the threat is and we have to have enough flexibility to deal with that threat; but it will be a NATO response and not a UK response.

Q150 John Smith: Finally, Chairman, when do we anticipate that the Stage 4 expansion will take place, and will we require more troops for that?
Air Marshal Sir Glenn Torpy: As I am sure the Committee understand Stage 3 expansion, the transfer of authority, is set against certain criteria. We anticipate that is going to happen probably in the late summer. Transfer of the Stage 4 area, again there are a number of conditions which will have to be met before that actually happens and NATO and the US coalition force at the moment will decide, depending on how the transition of Stage 3 goes, whether they are willing to transfer the Stage 4 area.

Q151 John Smith: They will decide the troop numbers?
Air Marshal Sir Glenn Torpy: Stage 4 effectively is a re-badging of the current US forces which are contained in that area underneath a NATO banner. I do not anticipate any significant change in the force levels which are contained in the Stage 4 area, which are predominantly US.
Dr Hutton: If I could just add to that, Chairman. We would be very keen for that transfer of authority to Stage 4 to take place during the tenure of HQ ARRC, as commander of ISAF, which ends in February next year.
Chairman: That was a very interesting answer you gave, Air Marshal, about a re-badging.

Q152 Mr Hancock: If I could ask a couple of brief questions relating to the relationship between ISAF and Operation Enduring Freedom. In the memorandum[10] you said that the command and control elements there still needed to be finalised and brought up to a better understanding. Can you tell us how that will be achieved, and when you would expect that to be in place? Are you satisfied that the "double-hatted" arrangements—for the US officer embedded in the ISAF command, your senior officers and, indeed, the British general who will command the whole operation—are clearly understood by all sides; and our general or NATO's general will not have to take second place to the American command structure back in the United States? Finally, can I ask about reinforcements? If reinforcements were required, do you believe that any other country (other than the UK) in NATO currently (excluding the Americans) would be able to furnish further troops if they were needed; or would it solely be down to the UK?
Air Marshal Sir Glenn Torpy: If I can deal, first of all, with the command control. I know the Committee has received a note following the last session which articulates that and things have moved on slightly in terms of clarification.[11] Basically, as the Committee is aware, Stage 1 and Stage 2 areas come under the current ISAF headquarters which is based around the Italian High Readiness Headquarters at the moment; and that will transfer to COMARRC in May of this year. The Stage 3 and Stage 4 areas are under the American coalition-led headquarters. The command and control structure which will be put in place in ARRC's tenure to transfer the Stage 3 and Stage 4 area, we hope, will basically consist of the three-star ISAF commander, which will be Lieutenant General David Richards, a British commander, and his headquarters. Underneath that will be three two-star officers: one will be responsible for managing all of the air resources; one will be responsible for stability operations, and that really focuses on the PRTs and enabling the PRTs. The final two-star officer will be responsible for security, and that will be a US two-star officer, and his responsibility under ISAF will be providing a secure environment under which the PRTs can carry out

[10] *Note:* See Ev 46.
[11] *Note:* See Ev 47.

their reconstruction and redevelopment work; but he will also be responsible for coordinating the activity of the relatively small US force which will be conducting counterterrorist operations. Within one headquarters we will have the ability to ensure that there is a proper level of de-confliction and coordination of both the ISAF force and the relatively small American force which will be conducting counterterrorist operations.

Q153 Mr Hancock: Before you answer the other parts of my question could I ask (as I asked the Secretary of State in questions in the House last week) about the use of NATO assets in Afghanistan. They will be solely at the discretion of the commander of ISAF, including the American-deployed NATO assets?
Air Marshal Sir Glenn Torpy: That is absolutely correct.

Q154 Mr Hancock: So he can make a decision to use those without having that countermanded by an American officer who says, "No, these are American assets and they are not to be deployed"?
Air Marshal Sir Glenn Torpy: That is exactly right.

Q155 Mr Hancock: That is fine. What about the second half of the question, about the reinforcements?
Air Marshal Sir Glenn Torpy: The point about the reinforcements, this is very much a job for NATO. It is a NATO commanded and generated force. COMISAF David Richards will clearly have the ability to move forces around Afghanistan to take account of a deteriorating security situation in any particular area. If he believes that he needs reinforcement from out of the theatre then he would go back to NATO and seek NATO to secure those forces from nations, exactly as it will be done during the Force Generation Process.

Q156 Mr Hancock: Are you saying, Air Marshal, that NATO troops or service personnel deployed in any part of Afghanistan can be deployed if necessary to Helmand Province?
Air Marshal Sir Glenn Torpy: This is where some national contingents will have caveats on the use of their forces. What NATO is seeking to do is ensure that there are an absolute minimum number of caveats, and that is what we are seeing from the bulk of the nations.

Q157 Mr Hancock: It would be helpful from this Committee's point of view and this report if we had that information about those countries which have caveated the use of NATO-deployed troops to Afghanistan to areas where only they will agree when they are deployed; because it makes the burden on the British troops deployed there greater, does it not?
Mr Ingram: I do not know whether that is information we are in a position to release. These are matters for individual governments. It is not a matter for this Committee to decide to comment on

the lay-down of other countries. We always say that it is a matter for that country. We do not comment publicly adversely on what is happening. It is a matter for those governments and for military commanders who have responsibility reporting to those governments, and ultimately the people of those countries to determine what it is they are seeking to do. I think everyone has learnt lessons about national caveats and we cannot deliver effective capabilities if they are too restrictive. All of those discussions go on all of the time to try and ensure there are no disconnects between what the overall mission is what a particular country may be putting in place.

Q158 Mr Hancock: It is a fair question, Minister, is it not? If NATO deployed troops in Afghanistan under a unified NATO commander and if some of the troops have restrictions placed upon them by their national government about where they can and cannot be deployed, and there are troops there from the UK who have an agreement that they will go anywhere and do anything, then the burden on reinforcements falls surely on the shoulders of those who will fall into that category. That is unfair if you are in a shared alliance, is it not?
Mr Ingram: What you are asking is a fair question although you have come to a conclusion. I do not think that is appropriate because that is not a given—what you have said. What we see all the time is all of the contributing nations having to talk about what it is they are doing, and if a particular country puts a condition on their participation then that has to be dealt with by the force commanders. They have to try and make sure that does not cause points of conflict and threat to other people. This is then into the military assessment of all of that and all the efforts are to minimise that and we do not have those worry lines. If you want to prove there are worry lines then I think you have got to take evidence from someone else in this, probably the most contributing nations.

Q159 Chairman: But the consequence might be, might it not, getting onto the question that John Smith asked, that there might be a need for reinforcement from the UK if other member nations of NATO are exercising these caveats?
Mr Ingram: Yes.
Dr Hutton: I would just make one point there. There is an over-the-horizon option already available for reinforcement in Afghanistan and that is the Strategic Reserve Force that NATO keeps for all its operational theatres. There is also the NATO Response Force for which reinforcement in Afghanistan is not a primary mission but *in extremis* you could use the NRF to reinforce Afghanistan. As you are well aware, that is a considerable force.
Mr Ingram: The point is that here we have a very concerted international focus in dealing with this problem. A lot of effort has been thrown into it. It is not just a military arrangement; it is all those other ingredients that come into play. People are not going in here for tokenistic reasons or simply flag-waving

to say, "Well, I'm here". This is a non-benign environment; the prospects of success are high if we get all of those aspects right. To talk about failure without any evidence that there is even an indication of failure and then saying, "What if?"—I know, if military planners then look at a range of factors, what we do not do is play out those issues in a public way. This is why that support mechanism is in place within NATO to achieve any immediate demand that may arise. It is easy to say that if such-and-such a thing applies you could then have strategic failure because those things do not apply, so therefore why examine it.

Q160 Mr Hancock: It is unfair of the Minister to allege that we are talking about failure. We are here to ask legitimate questions and they were, in my opinion, legitimate questions. Nobody in this room, to my knowledge, has talked about "failure". We all want it to succeed, Minister. It is wrong of you to imply that we do not.
Mr Ingram: I have given my answer.

Q161 Mr Hamilton: For the record, could you tell us where in Helmand the UK's deployment will take place and what its objectives are?
Air Marshal Sir Glenn Torpy: If I go back first of all to what are the ISAF objectives, because clearly we would be under their command, those I think fall down into three areas: first of all, what we are aiming to do is to maintain and establish a secure environment throughout Afghanistan to enable the reconstruction and stabilisation of the country. What we are going to be focused on, on the military side, is, first of all, providing a secure environment; and, secondly, capacity-building with the Afghan National Army and supporting also development of the Afghan National Police. In doing that we are enabling the PRT activity, which is focussed on reconstruction and development activities. I think those are the broad principles of what the UK force is going to be contributing to. In terms of where we are actually located, we will have our main logistic and aviation located at Kandahar airfield, which is the main airfield in the region, in the south. That is also where the multinational brigade headquarters is located and, as the Committee is aware, the first rotation will be commanded by the Canadians—and they took command on 1 March. Our forces in Helmand, the PRT, will be located at Lashkar Gar, and that is going to be about 100 strong with a mix of military, FCO, DFID and US representatives from the State Departments and their Agriculture Ministry as well, and there will be appropriate force protection. Then we are also located at two other locations, Camp Bastion where we will be training the Afghan National Army, which is their main location; and another forward-operating base at Gereshk.

Q162 Mr Hamilton: Mindful of the fact that the Americans (whom we will be going in to replace in many cases) will spend millions of pounds in infrastructure and building a substantial amount of buildings and so on, when we go in there, will we be going under the same amount of money which will allow us to do that reconstruction that we talk about? Are you talking about Camp Bastion, or are you talking about an area where the British troops are going in and replacing, as I understand it, the United States? The United States has a substantial amount of money it has been putting into the area.
Mr Ingram: You mean for their own troops?

Q163 Mr Hamilton: No, for the people involved there and to help the Afghanistan people.
Mr Ingram: What was committed in terms of the London conference again was a very significant sum of money—£500 million, I think—over the three-year period overall and not for the south. DFID, from our own country, are contributing £30 million into that area; the $100 million which the US were committed to remains for another year at least. There is more money going in and the way that is spent will be driven by how best we can get a good return from it, in the sense of alternative livelihoods and in terms of what it is people need—is it roads, is it infrastructure or whatever else? In one sense, if you are producing alternative crop livelihood you have got to get the crop to market so all these things have to be taken into consideration. It is really not, in one sense, a matter for me—although clearly there is good cross-departmental working in all of this. The definition of this and the way that will be delivered is really a matter for DFID and other agencies that they will be supporting.

Q164 Mr Hamilton: But that has a direct effect in relation to how our troops function?
Mr Ingram: Absolutely.

Q165 Mr Hamilton: It is important if we are talking in terms of reconstruction and winning the hearts and minds that the question really is: are we in a position where we can do that and will we have the wherewithal i.e. finance to establish that?
Mr Ingram: There are significant additional contributions going in because it is recognised that has to be achieved.

Q166 Mr Hamilton: Finally, have we learnt lessons from Iraq that we can transfer across to Afghanistan in relation to winning the hearts and minds of the people there? Minister, I am mindful of the pictures that came up in Iraq where we have seen the American troops stood there armed up to the teeth, and then we have seen the British troops with their helmets off in the initial stages. Are we in a position where we can downsize as part of winning the hearts and the minds of the people in that area?
Mr Ingram: Really it becomes a matter for the commanders in the field as to how they then interface with the people and the potential threat. These are very fine judgements that we ask them to perform. I think we have a very significant measure of success and we do up the protection and we lower it and we up it and all the time people are trained to get to that point of engagement. That type of

measure and that type of approach can only succeed when you have the willingness amongst the people themselves to so engage. If the threat level is high then the full commanders will not put the people at risk.

Air Marshal Sir Glenn Torpy: I would just add, because I happened to have been in Afghanistan last week, I was walking around Lashkar Gar with our PRT people whom we have got down there as part of the initial team, and I went and talked to some of the Afghans. I think consent is high and their two major concerns are security and employment. That is what we have got to deliver for them.

Q167 Chairman: There are some questions I would have liked to have asked about the Spring Supplementary Estimates and costs.

Mr Ingram: I would have loved to have answered them!

Q168 Chairman: I am sure you would, Minister. Instead you will be able to answer them in a letter because I will write to you; but I will need an answer within the next couple of days. I will write today if that is okay. If you could do your utmost to get me an answer within the next couple of days.

Mr Ingram: Yes.[12]

Chairman: Moving onto the equipment that the Armed Forces will have.

Q169 Mr Lancaster: Minister, just to look at the change of threat really and, in particular, from Improvised Explosive Devices. Traditionally IEDs were improvised claymores or covert mines which would only really be effective against soft-skinned vehicles, but in recent times we have seen the use of shaped chargers where plastic explosive superheats the soft metal white copper and then drills the molten slug through armour. This is very much an increase in the threat. Are you confident that we are sending the right quantity of armoured vehicles to Afghanistan; and has there been any review in view of this increase in threat from the use of shaped chargers?

Mr Ingram: Addressing your second point first, we are always alert to what the new threat will be. Even in terms of the means of delivery of it countermeasures are being developed all the time, and I know you will appreciate it is not appropriate to talk about and the efficacy of how we tackle all of that. If the threat changes and it is new to us then we very quickly analyse it, and if it is technically possible we very quickly find a countermeasure. If we do not find a technical solution other approaches have to be adopted to minimise that threat. I think we have got to live in the real world, that it is impossible to remove every threat. We cannot have a perfect environment. Are there vulnerabilities: probably. Do we try to minimise those vulnerabilities: 100% as they are identified. We take care of our people very high, and where lessons have

to be learned they are learned. If there is need for additional equipment or new protective measures then they are brought forward if it can be proven that they will prove to be effective. There is no point spending money simply as a reaction. It has got to be proven that it will deliver that protection which we are then seeking to apply. In terms of what we have on the ground, in terms of the right type of equipment, this has all been analysed. What the commanders seek they will be given. Are they stretched at times? Yes, they are. All forces find themselves in this position, not just the UK; even the mighty US will find itself in those stretched positions as well. What we have got to seek to do is identify the threat levels, hear what the commanders are saying through the Chain of Command and then, if remedies can be found, put those remedies in place.

Q170 Mr Lancaster: Can I press you on that, because technology is not really the answer. Shaped chargers have been around since the Second World War, and everybody knows what the threat is.

Mr Ingram: I was talking about the method of delivery as well.

Q171 Mr Lancaster: The point really is that recently commanders in Iraq are concerned, and have voiced their concern in things like *Defence News*, that we are simply not sending enough armour to Afghanistan. The question is specifically: has there been a recent review of the amount of armour that has been sent to Afghanistan in light of the current threat?

Mr Ingram: What we have done is we have defined what it is we need in terms of equipment and people. Remembering there is a very significant air component in all of this, a very powerful potent force has been put in place to provide greater agility, to keep the threat more remote from the direct attack. I am very reluctant to go into "vulnerabilities" because there are points where, if we discuss things, all it does is give to those willing to carry out the attacks some indication of where the weak points are. I do not think that serves our people in any way whatsoever in this. I would say to you, with all respect, we cannot be perfect, and do not ask us to be perfect. We will get as near to that as we possibly can, but we do not live in a perfect world, no Armed Forces do.

Q172 Mr Lancaster: I am not asking you to be perfect. I am simply asking in the light of recent events in Iraq and the increased threat, has there been a review of the amount of armoured vehicles being sent to Afghanistan? That is all I am asking.

Air Marshal Sir Glenn Torpy: Yes, there has. Without going into details of the IED threat, for the reasons the Minister has explained, we keep that under continuous review. As you mentioned, to defeat that sort of threat relies on equipment, tactics, training and procedures; and you will know that from our experience in Iraq. I believe we are sending

---

[12] *Note:* See Defence Committee Fourth Report, Session 2005–06. Costs of Peacekeeping in Iraq and Afghanistan: Spring Supplementary Estimate 2005–06.

the right force to match the threat which exists at the moment. If the threat changes we will then have to review the full structure.

Q173 Mr Havard: Part of what is generating the question is whether or not there are enough Warriors, whether you are sending Warriors and whether or not the changes that are happening in terms of the support system for the Warrior are actually going to be sufficient to achieve the trick in both Afghanistan and Iraq. When we are talking about armoured vehicles we are largely talking about Warriors.

Air Marshal Sir Glenn Torpy: I think the other thing which has to be taken into account is the environment in which you are putting the force. At the moment Afghanistan does not have main battle tanks; it does not have armoured fighting vehicles. I am not convinced that if those were put into that environment we would maintain the sort of environment that we are looking to develop—the security environment—and also the reconstruction effort. I go back to the point about maintaining the consent of the Afghan people so that we can actually carry out the mission. That has to be balanced against the risks we are taking against the threat as well.

Mr Ingram: The core message here is, yes, we have analysed the threat; and, yes, we have defined what force is required to deal with it; we are confident there is a sufficiency of that. If that threat changes then we would subject that to further consideration to see what could be done to deal with that.

Q174 Chairman: There was an article in *Defence News* this morning in which it was stated that army commanders had asked for new-wheeled vehicles to be sent to Afghanistan. What you said a few minutes ago was, what commanders seek they will be given. Would you reassure us that what you have just said remains?

Mr Ingram: I also said "through the Chain of Command". I know you understand this, Chairman, if it comes to ministerial decision the big filter is: what are the military saying; what are the requirements; what are the priorities? We have a very good close relationship within the Ministry of Defence, which has been there well before my time, and probably before your time when you were a minister, in terms of understanding each other as to what can be done. When I say it is through the Chain of Command, it is a question of the experienced heads analysing what it is that has been sought. Sometimes what is sought may not be available. Therefore, how then do we deal with the new threat that has been identified? It may well even be that we do not have the technical capability to do it. We may not have the support capable to do it and put in place and it could take you months before you get to that point. I could give examples of previous conflicts where the demand is there and the supply is not—not because of unwillingness to deliver where you are purchasing it from but because of other

manufacturing issues. There are a lot of issues out there and there are a lot of subtleties to that. If it becomes a priority then we seek to meet it.

Q175 Chairman: One of the things that inserts itself into the Chain of Command somehow always seems to be the Treasury.

Mr Ingram: That is genuinely unfair. The Treasury have a very important role to play. That is to hold us all to account as spending departments and that is a difficult job as well, but they have to say, "What is it you are seeking?" because the money that is being committed is not being committed elsewhere and every other department is claiming access to that. They have to prioritise as well but they have not shown resistance when we look at the sums that we have contributed both to Iraq and Afghanistan.

Q176 Mr Hancock: Could you give an indication to the Committee whether you believe, as the political responsible person, that all reasonable requests made by commanders on the ground arrive at you for new equipment or for extra equipment; or are they filtered by other officers before they get to you, because the suggestion that the Chairman made was that there was a genuine request for more wheeled vehicles to be put into Afghanistan and that came from a commander on the ground. You said immediately, "That has to go through the Chain of Command." I am interested to know whether the Chain of Command says no before it gets to you. That is why they end up being requested through newspapers rather than the Chain of Command.

Mr Ingram: I have not had time to read *The Defence News* this morning and I am always a bit wary of anything that I read given the fact that in one newspaper there is a glaring headline that does not even relate to the answer I gave. Interpretation by journalists can be—I will be careful what I say here, but they can over-interpret; they can deliberately interpret. If they have a particular angle, they can take you down a particular route and ignore the facts, or they never even ask the centre source—not the person who may have made a side comment—because they would rather have the story than the truth. We are always chasing rumours, stories and things which are already being addressed, so I am not accepting the scenario as being a given until I have seen what has been said and how it has been addressed.

Q177 Mr Hancock: Have you, Minister, turned down any requests for extra equipment for our troops to be deployed in Afghanistan from commanders?

Mr Ingram: No.

Q178 Mr Hancock: If I could return to the air capability, you said earlier that there was a significant air component there. The Secretary of State, on 26 January, mentioned providing fast jets and transport aircraft for the Helmand deployment. What capabilities have been asked for, what has been provided and who by?

Air Marshal Sir Glenn Torpy: You have to look at the whole air package both in terms of the rotary wing aviation and the fixed wing aircraft which are available in Afghanistan as well. We put what I think is a pretty robust package together on the aviation side. As the Committee is aware, we have eight Apache going, six Chinooks and four Lynx. There are also upwards of more than 20 American helicopters which will be operating in the southern region, together with some Dutch helicopters as well. In terms of mobility and fire power on the rotary wing aviation, I think we are pretty well served. In terms of fixed wing air assets, again the Committee is aware we have six Harriers based down at Kandahar and the Dutch have committed six F16 in the force generation process as well. Up at Bagram the US have a number of A10s and out of theatre there is a range of US resources which they have committed to Afghanistan as well in terms of intelligence surveillance, reconnaissance aircraft, air to air refuelling aircraft and strategic aircraft such as B52s which can carry out a precision attack. Overall, there is a robust air package. It is all commanded through the coalition air component operation centre in Al Udeid in Qatar, where there are NATO and UK officers embedded in that, to ensure that the air is properly coordinated for Afghanistan and that US resources predominantly which could be used in Iraq or Afghanistan can be properly prioritised.

Q179 Mr Hancock: Are you absolutely sure that the Americans will continue to provide the sort of support they have done? You are nodding so you have obviously had that discussion. You are satisfied that our troops will not find themselves somewhat isolated because of the withdrawal of American aircraft from Afghanistan?
Air Marshal Sir Glenn Torpy: No. I go back to one of my earlier statements that the US forces in the stage four area are coming under ISAF so it is in the US interest to ensure that their air resources are available to support the ISAF mission which they will be.

Q180 Mr Hancock: Is it still, in your opinion, the easiest way to transport large numbers of troops around Afghanistan, by aircraft?
Air Marshal Sir Glenn Torpy: Given the distances and the terrain, a combination of fixed wing air transport and rotary wing is one of the most practical ways, given that there is only one major road.

Q181 Mr Hancock: Is it the safest way?
Air Marshal Sir Glenn Torpy: It is also probably the safest way as well.

Q182 Robert Key: I thought the Harrier GR7 squadron in Kandahar was going to be replaced in June.
Air Marshal Sir Glenn Torpy: What the Secretary of State said was that we kept the Harriers there until June because that was when the runway at Kandahar was going to be refurbished and the refurbishment of the runway would be complete. At that stage, we would review the K30 to see if there were sufficient NATO resources to provide an adequate level of air support and we are just in the process of doing exactly that.

Q183 Robert Key: Are all the Hercules deployed in Afghanistan fitted with full defensive aid suites?
Air Marshal Sir Glenn Torpy: They are.

Q184 Robert Key: Can you define what you mean by "full"?
Air Marshal Sir Glenn Torpy: They have adequate defensive aids to match the threat that we are going to face in Afghanistan, without going into the detail of the defensive aids.

Q185 Robert Key: This is quite important because yesterday in the House of Lords Lord Drayson said in column 524 that we use aircraft only when they have the appropriate defensive aid suites. Later on, in answer to Lord Luke, he said that the aircraft go into those areas having in all cases the defensive aid suites that they require. Can you confirm that in 2004–05 the programme to equip the 15J Hercules with the latest generation defensive aid suites was cancelled?
Air Marshal Sir Glenn Torpy: I cannot confirm that.
Mr Ingram: We will write to you on that.[13] I do not have the detail. I used the word "vulnerability" earlier. We are up against a very clever, intelligent enemy. The more we want to examine in minutiae everything that we are doing, the more we are telling those who are going to pose a threat. I am not saying they are not legitimate or fair questions. I am telling you why there is a reluctance to expose too much knowledge. The knowledge may be interesting to you but it is much more interesting to those who pose a threat.

Q186 Robert Key: It is not just of interest to this Committee; it is of interest to all the military personnel involved and their families as well as the taxpayer. I suggest that there is a case for moving into closed session to explore some of these in detail because of the evidence that has been reaching the Defence Committee.
Mr Ingram: If it is evidence reaching the Defence Committee, on the basis of cooperation and willingness to give best information, we need the evidence. Let us make sure it is evidence and not tittle tattle.
Robert Key: I do not think that is a sensible thing for the Minister to have said.
Mr Hancock: Can I ask the Air Marshal to clarify his answer to Mr Key? Mr Key asked a specific question. He said, "Were the C130 Hercules deployed to Afghanistan fitted with full defensive aid suites?" You said, "Yes." You went on to say that there was a qualitative nature. They were adequate for what they were expected to do. I want to know if full is the same as adequate.

---

[13] *Note:* Awaiting response.

Q187 Robert Key: It is not, is it?

Air Marshal Sir Glenn Torpy: There is a range of defensive aids that you can put on any aircraft. There are radar warning receivers, missile warning receivers and other defensive aids and I would not want to go into the details of those. We will never put an aircraft into Afghanistan which does not have a defensive aid suite that we think is capable of taking on the threat which they may be faced with.

Q188 Chairman: It has been suggested that we should move into closed session which we will consider doing towards the end of this at about 10 to 12.

Mr Ingram: I am not sure that we have the answers you are seeking.

Chairman: You may not have the answers but in the questions which we will be able to put in closed session you will be able to go away and think about those answers.

Q189 John Smith: Are we satisfied that the forward support for fixed wing is adequate at Kandahar for maintaining and repairing the Harrier?

Air Marshal Sir Glenn Torpy: Absolutely, and we have been operating them there since September 2004.

Q190 Mr Havard: When I visited 16 Air Assault Brigade, they were quite clear to me about their own particular concept of air manoeuvre and what they wanted to try and do and how they were going to do it. It is a different way of working given that we are using the Apaches in the way that we are in particular circumstances. The question is about tactical lift and it partly relates to the question earlier on about armour. It is a question of how you manoeuvre on the ground what are essentially going to be infantry troops supported by air. There are a number of assets that you have described, both rotary and fixed, that are supposed to help to do that. How is that combination going to work with the ground assets as well? Are you confident that this process of getting the people to the right place, at the right time, in the right way and evacuated from it is sufficient to do the job?

Mr Ingram: This is not an experiment or a test. I know you have spoken to those commanders who have thought long and hard about the mix of the assets to have and how best they can utilise them to achieve their objective. As ever, they will learn on the ground. It is on the basis of what is the threat; how has it been assessed? Does that change things and how do they then reshape what our response would be to all of that? There is nothing new, I would guess—I am not a military person—in terms of air assets to other assets we have.

Chairman: Because of the time, we need to get on to the issue of narcotics.

Q191 Linda Gilroy: I wonder if Mr Holland could give us a very quick overview and tell us about ADIDU, how it is staffed, what its budget is and what its purpose is?

Mr Holland: ADIDU is a cross-departmental unit. It was set up a year ago on 1 February with approval from the Prime Minister. It is an interdepartmental unit. We have staff in it from the Foreign Office, the Ministry of Defence, DFID, HMRC soon to be SOCA and the Home Office. It was deliberately put together as an interdepartmental unit because it recognised that the counter narcotics issue and the approach we needed to take needed to bring together all the resources across government. We have a counterpart organisation, the British Embassy Drugs Team, based in the embassy in Kabul, who are in a sense the implementing agency on the ground. Our role is to set the strategy and coordinate the UK approach to counter narcotics in Afghanistan and also to coordinate and work with international partners on that because we are the key G8 partner nation, as you will be aware, on counter narcotics, in the key G8 partner nations. In terms of resources, the government has committed £270 million over three years starting this financial year to the counter narcotics issue in Afghanistan. Of that, 130 million will be provided by DFID towards primarily alternative livelihoods programmes. The remaining £140 million which we are responsible for overseeing is provided by the other stakeholder departments.

Q192 Linda Gilroy: You have spoken about the role, but the Committee will probably be interested to know more about whether that is going to concentrate on breaking the narcotics supply chain or on eradicating the supply.

Mr Holland: Our role and our policy are very much in support of the government of Afghanistan's national drug control strategy which was published at the London conference. They identified four main priorities which are targeting the trafficker and the trade, so disrupting the networks, building strong and diversified legal livelihoods, building strong government institutions and tackling the demand side, because there is an increasing demand problem within Afghanistan. In terms of our own priorities, we are particularly focusing on the first three of those. 70% of the resources that ADIDU is overseeing are being targeted at the trafficker and the trade, building effective police forces and criminal justice institutions. DFID's programme, 130 million, is primarily focused on alternative livelihoods and the rest of what we are putting in is mainly focused on building government institutions, both central and local government. We are putting a small element into supporting the elimination campaign. That is primarily led by the US. The areas that we are particularly focusing on is providing targeting information to make sure that any eradication is carried out in areas where alternative livelihoods already exist, so it is targeting those we describe as the greedy, not the needy, and supporting the UN Office for Drugs and Crime and the government of Afghanistan to verify that eradication has taken place.

Q193 Linda Gilroy: On the building of institutions, what is your assessment of the capability and willingness of the judicial system to prosecute those who are involved in drug trafficking particularly?

Mr Holland: It is beginning to develop. It is at a pretty early stage. We have particularly concentrated on building a specific strand within the overall criminal justice institutions to focus on counter narcotics. The elements of that have included, first of all, a new counter narcotics law passed in December which sets very clearly the legal framework for that and the responsibilities. We have also, through the support of the UN Office for Drugs and Crime, trained a criminal justice task force. That is a task force of about 80 people, prosecutors, investigators and judges. Within that there has been a separate division of the central court set up to specifically prosecute drugs cases. Since it was established in May, it has had about 90 convictions. It is currently pursuing about 240 cases so it is really accelerating its effort. We have not yet seen the first conviction of a really significant trafficker. There have been some low to medium value traffickers but at the moment it is pursuing its first case of a significant trafficker.

Q194 Linda Gilroy: Do the intelligence and the experience of the court system suggest that the Taliban is now involved in the narcotics trade?

Mr Holland: We have not seen direct experience until very recently of those kinds of links. There are some indications, particularly in the south, that the Taliban have been encouraging farmers to grow poppy this year and offering them protection against law enforcement forces, yes.

Q195 Linda Gilroy: On the alternative livelihoods, there is big investment going into those. Have you looked at the arguments to have licensed opium production as proposed by the Senlis Council? Do they have any merit?

Mr Holland: Yes. We have looked at this in some detail and I can give the Committee a paper that analyses this. We did some analysis of this before the Senlis Council's report. We share the view of the government of Afghanistan that, at this time, it is not an appropriate solution for Afghanistan. We would identify two main reasons. The one which the government of Afghanistan is particularly concerned about is that, if you have a licit license system, there are not sufficient control mechanisms yet in place to prevent diversion from that. What you would have is a risk of not reducing the illicit trade but potentially increasing it. The other aspect is the economic side of it. At the moment, farmers receive around $100 per kilo from traffickers for their opium crop. The nearest comparable country that currently has a licit system is India. For them the greatest price that farmers receive is about $35 a kilo. An licit system would not compete directly with an illicit system. On both the economic side and on the control side, we do not think at this stage a licensing system is appropriate.

Q196 Mr Havard: We know from descriptions you have given us that the NATO rules of engagement allow people to detain someone. The question about what happens to them subsequently is a matter of debate and discussion country by country and for the Afghan government to establish. You say that you were negotiating a process with them to do that. Has that now been concluded? Can you say something about what it would be?

Mr Ingram: It has not been concluded but we are coming to the conclusions of it. These are detailed matters. It relates to the applicability of domestic UK law, defined as English law, our international obligations, what is permissible or not under the Security Council resolutions. They are very detailed issues to be addressed. If I was asked if I am confident we will get there, I think we will get there but we are not there yet. We know the importance of getting this in place as soon as possible because we now have a considerable number of troops already there who may find themselves in the position of having to deal with this.

Q197 Mr Havard: This operates at a number of levels. We are concerned obviously for the human rights of the people who are interdicted as well as the situation of the forces themselves and where they rest in terms of their legal protection in these circumstances. That is the main driver for us, to be sure that there is clarity both for the individual soldier in this circumstance and through the Chain of Command as to exactly where they sit in relation to their duties, what the processes are and that they are properly carried out, monitored and so on.

Mr Ingram: Absolutely. I give you that commitment. This is uppermost in our minds, to make sure that our people are not put into a position of uncertainty as to how to deal with it because there are too many critics out there who will have a go at our people without even beginning to understand the complexity of the environment which they are in. Therefore, we owe it to them to give the best clarity. There are two key players in this of course in terms of our own government and the Afghan government and we are working our way to a conclusion in all of this.

Q198 Chairman: We have suggested going into private session. If the Committee is agreed we will do that.

Air Marshal Sir Glenn Torpy: Could I clarify on defensive aid suites? Maybe I did not make myself completely clear. Defensive aid suites mean exactly what they say. There is a range of capabilities which are brigaded under that. Some are for warning and some are for countering the threats which are then picked up by those systems. All of our aircraft will have an appropriate suite of those capabilities to match the threat that our intelligence indicates is going to be faced in Afghanistan.

Chairman: I think we still have some questions we would like to ask.

Resolved, That the Committee should not sit in private.

The witnesses gave further oral evidence.

Asterisks denote that part of the oral evidence which, for security reasons, has not been reported at the request of the Ministry of Defence and with the agreement of the Committee.

Q199 Chairman: Is the Committee content that the specialist adviser should stay? (Agreed) Minister, can you confirm that those in the room behind you are from the Ministry of Defence?
Mr Ingram: Yes.
Chairman: We were asking questions about defensive aid suites and we would like to ask some questions about explosive suppressant foam.

Q200 Robert Key: It seems to me unlikely that we are going to have enough of the model K Hercules which definitely has the latest generation DA suites and we are going to use more Js which are not upgraded. Evidence has been given to the Committee that there was a programme to equip 15 of the Js with the latest generation of DAS but the programme was cancelled. Is that true? Therefore, does that account for the fact that we have also been told that some of the pilots are most concerned because they are not clear in Afghanistan whether they should be flying high where they will still be able to be hit by some missile or low, hedge hopping. We have evidence from other Members of Parliament that there has been hedge hopping because pilots have not been clear whether they should be high or low because they do not have full defensive aid suites.
Mr Ingram: You say that evidence has been given. Has it been given in public session to the Committee?

Q201 Robert Key: No.
Mr Ingram: If it was in public session, my worries and caveats would have been there. I do not know the source of the evidence. I do not know whether we should be privy to where it is coming from. If it is evidence, then I would guess that it has to be questioned. Has it been questioned or is it just information that has been given?
Robert Key: I would say it is credible but, Chairman, it is for you to decide.
John Smith: It is single source.
Chairman: It is from Lord Hamilton.
Robert Key: And the pilot.
Mr Havard: It is Nigel Gilbert.[14]

Q202 Chairman: He has been on television saying these things.
Mr Ingram: We will need to take on board the question. We do not have the answer here. We will try and get you the answer. We will have to see what the allegation is and therefore what the decision line is because there may well be a process where this has actually been considered. Someone within the

---

bounds of the system may say it has been rejected but it may not have been rejected. Therefore, maybe "tittle tattle" was the wrong phrase but it is not authoritative because it does not accord with the full processes that are currently under way. What we will always seek to do is to ensure that we give the best protection to our people. That is not always easily achievable. It is not always something we can deliver tomorrow and therefore that is why I used the word "vulnerabilities", because the hard logic of what has perhaps been argued by some people is that until everything is done nothing is done. I am not saying those around this table but others use this argument that, if there is a risk that could result in a loss of life, we should not be committing our forces before reducing or removing that risk. That is not humanly possible for any modern Armed Forces. I hope the Committee understands that what we have to do is to minimise that risk.

Q203 Robert Key: The Minister needs to understand we are entirely on his side. This goes back to the question about the Treasury. If, because of financial constraints, you are unable to upgrade the Js, we think that is something which is regrettable.
Mr Ingram: It will not be the Treasury necessarily. It could also be our prioritisation because we have to balance how much money we have to spend and what we are going to do with it, recognising by not doing something that there is an element of risk associated with it. How dangerous or significant that risk is then has to be considered. It is easy to say it is the Treasury but we have responsibility for managing our resources.
Mr Jenkins: I did not want to stop us going into private session but I did not realise how flimsy the response was. I am not prepared to ask the Minister to comment on a letter. What I am prepared to do is to give the Minister the letter and any other information we have and say, "Go away and come back with your report" and then I can crucify him if necessary on the answer, but not at the present time. We have to ask him to go away and come up with his best answer with regard to these claims and then we can go through with it but, at the present time, we are just talking for the sake of talking.
Chairman: We have had allegations put to us which I think we probably want to investigate.

Q204 Mr Hamilton: I agree with Brian. I am surprised that we went into private session to discuss one comment. The Minister made a comment just before we went into private session: "Give me the information and I will give a response." I have been on several committees since I came here in 2001 and two major committees and I have never seen anything conducted in this way. We are not trying to trap the Minister; we are trying to engage in finding information. Robert makes the point that we are in a supportive role but I would far rather, if we are going to be asking questions, that the information be given to the appropriate authority and then we go into private session and discuss the detail of what that is about.

Mr Ingram: What happens to the information we give? If this is in private session, it cannot surface?

Chairman: That is fully accepted.

Mr Hancock: I am not here to defend you, Chairman, but I do not think you had a choice at the time. You were in the course of a discussion here. You were already seeking to clarify the responses you gave, Air Marshal, and that is why you said what you did. You had obviously reflected on what had been said and you wanted to clarify that, so there were some real difficulties. It would have been wrong for this to have continued in open session and I do not think you had an alternative, Chairman. The point I would like to make is not even to you, Minister, or to you, Air Marshal, because I do not think it is fair to ask you this question. It is for your colleagues in the Air Force to answer the questions because I have spoken to this man on two occasions and he says that there have been requests made through the Chain of Command that have never arrived at ministers' desks.

John Smith: There are always requests.

Q205 Mr Hancock: These are about people flying large numbers of service personnel. Some of them were killed in an accident. We heard from our colleague in the House of Lords yesterday that there is now a different version of events in the bringing down of that Hercules and these people are—

Mr Ingram: There is only one version of events and that is the BOI. Anyone who speculates has not done the technical analysis. The BOI is out there and therefore, if you are talking about the suppression, this was asked for and never came up through the system. When was the request made? This is not evidence; this is information. When was it asked for? Who suppressed it? Who made the decision not to proceed? That individual can say what everyone knew about this and answer to all the problems. That is not the conclusion of the BOI and therefore there are a lot of assumptions in there that you have not interrogated.

Q206 Robert Key: That is what we are doing.

Mr Ingram: You are basing it upon someone saying something but you have not put that person on the spot and said, "Where were you at the time this was done? Were you part of that decision making chain or did someone tell you this?" There is a range of questions. Is this a credible set of information?

Robert Key: Yes.

Mr Havard: I do not know whether it is credible but it is single source.

Robert Key: No; two.

Mr Havard: I do not know about Lord What's-His-Face. I have never heard of him.

Robert Key: He is a former defence minister.

Q207 Mr Havard: Maybe he is. We have two letters from one individual who is an ex-pilot, who alleges that this asset is vulnerable in a number of different ways. He says that it does not have the appropriate defensive aid suite on it of the type necessary for looking at rate based seeker heads or missiles and so on. He makes a comment about that. He makes a comment about the armour possibility in the aircraft, where they have to sit on chains and sit on ceramic plates in case they get shot in the bum. He makes the point about there not being sufficient process in order to deal with the foam problem in the wings if he gets shot down. He then goes on to talk about recovery and rescue and not enough support for that. It moves from the vulnerability of the asset to how you retrieve or protect the asset and so on. All of these are issues that he raises. Whether or not any of them have any validity or how much there is on each one I do not know. I would like to give you all this information so you can go away and look at it and give us some answers. Until then, it is only one source, as far as I am concerned, alleging that all these things are true.

Mr Ingram: ***[15] I do not know this individual who is saying this but all he is doing is pointing up the vulnerabilities. Is there an answer to it? Possibly. Can we deliver it? Possibly. When are we going to do it? We have to decide is it worthwhile doing in terms of the age of the aircraft, whether it is technically possible and what it means in terms of the fleet. If the view is that there is a risk associated with this and someone's life may be lost, that is the nature of conflict. It weighs heavy on all of the minds who make those decisions. There are risks in everything that we do. We have to decide can we find an answer to it and, if we talk about this in the public arena as this gentleman is doing, he is effectively saying, "Why not have a go at the bad guys?"

Chairman: I want to agree with what David Hamilton said that it is no part of this Committee's work to try to trap a minister. I do not think that we have been trying to do that, but I do believe that there have been allegations which have been made which we do need to get to the bottom of. It is the view of this Committee that we should send you all this correspondence and ask for your answers. If I may say so, you have done the points you have made no damage whatsoever by the way you have put matters in the last 10 minutes. Thank you very much indeed. I am very grateful to you for staying later than 12 o'clock. Thank you very much.

---

[15] Not printed.

Written evidence

Memorandum from the British American Security Information Council (BASIC)

1. INTRODUCTION

1.1 The British-led Allied Rapid Reaction Corps (ARRC) will take command of the International Security Assistance Force (ISAF) at a unique and critical time. Afghanistan has experienced an upsurge in violence in 2005. This violence emanates from a mix of continued warlordism and Taliban and Al Qaeda remnants becoming more organised and perhaps more desperate. The North Atlantic Treaty Organisation (NATO) is under pressure to take on a combat role either under, or in conjunction with, the US-led Operation Enduring Freedom. This submission raises issues that the UK government will need to consider carefully before ISAF joins Operation Enduring Freedom in undertaking a broader combat role in Afghanistan.

1.2 The submission begins with a brief overview of the security environment. Taking into account the current environment, it is our contention that Afghanistan is in need of strengthened peace operations rather than a greater investment in combat operations. This reasoning is also based on the possible ramifications of NATO taking over Operation Enduring Freedom or at least taking on a greater combat role. The second part of the submission explores a series of brief scenarios for the Defence Committee and other relevant parties to consider before next spring. *If NATO takes on Operation Enduring Freedom or a full-fledged combat role in conjunction with that operation, the alliance could jeopardize ISAF peace operations*.

2. THE SECURITY ENVIRONMENT IN AFGHANISTAN

2.1 Afghanistan is witnessing its highest level of violence in several years. While Taliban and Al Qaeda still threaten southern and eastern Afghanistan, heavily armed warlords and militia commanders pose a violent threat throughout the country.[1] A persistently weak security sector permits this violence to continue.

2.2. Deaths from militant-related violence topped 1,200 from January to August 2005. Moreover, insurgents and militia are pinpointing their attacks at the redeveloping security sector. Six hundred Afghan police died violently between 9 October 2004 and 16 May 2005.[2] After recent parliamentary elections, the Taliban attacked an army training centre and killed at least 12 Afghans, most of whom were army officers. The attack took place near a base for NATO-led peace operations. It was the worst suicide attack in Kabul since the overthrow of the Taliban in 2001.[3]

2.3 There are several plausible reasons for the increase in violence in the past 12 months or so. Most observers expected an increase in violence before the September 2005 parliamentary elections. Also, Al Qaeda and the Taliban may have sharpened their tactics after four years of combat experience with coalition forces. Some analysts have also argued that Taliban and Al Qaeda numbers are dwindling and, therefore, that they are becoming more desperate and launching as many attacks as they can muster before time runs out. In addition, warlords, militia commanders and common criminals have been able to prey off of the market for poppy production and the absence of strong and legitimate security structures.

2.4 While the war with the Taliban and Al Qaeda is continuing, Afghans are more concerned with the problem of widespread warlordism and crime. Crime has increased significantly in recent years. The increase in crime moved protestors in March 2005 to call for the resignation of Kandahar's governor.[4] When questioned by the International Republican Institute in the fall of 2004, 50% of those Afghans polled said that the disarmament of commanders and warlords was their biggest concern. This concern ranked above worries about economic development and Al Qaeda and Taliban. But rather surprisingly perhaps, only 7% of those polled said strengthening the national army and police was their priority.[5]

2.5 These poll results seem to oversimplify a complicated and interconnected security problem in Afghanistan. It is hard to see how warlords and commanders will surrender their arms and shady careers in crime without better alternatives that can come only from an improved economic environment. Likewise, the Taliban and Al Qaeda are unlikely to be defeated and will gain more adherents so long as Afghanistan depends on foreigners for security and aid. While the Japanese-led disarmament and demobilization effort has made some inroads, the country is unlikely to make much more progress in disarming the various militias and armed factions without its own effective security forces. *Afghanistan will be hard pressed to make a strong economic recovery if it fails to escape from violence perpetrated by Taliban, Al Qaeda, and especially*

---

[1] Miller, Laurel and Perito, Robert, "Establishing the Rule of Law in Afghanistan", *United States Institute of Peace Special Report* 117, March 2004.

[2] O'Hanlon, Michael, and Kamp, Nina, "Afghanistan Index: Tracking Variables of Reconstruction and Security in Post-Taliban Afghanistan", The Brookings Institution, 15 September 2005, URL http://www.brookings.edu/fp/research/projects/southasia/afghanistanindex.pdf, p 2.

[3] "UN Curbs Staff After Kabul Bomb; Taliban Vows More", Reuters via *Khaleej Times*, 29 September 2005.

[4] Tarzi, Amin, "Afghan Demonstrations Test Warlords-Turned-Administrators", RFE/RL Reports, Vol 4, No 9, 11 March 2005.

[5] O'Hanlon, Michael and Kamp, Nina, "Afghanistan Index", *OpCit*; 17,100 Afghans interviewed in 26 Afghan provinces and in Pakistan, "International Republican Institute Election Day Survey", 13 November 2004, URL http://www.iri.org/pdfs/survey102104.ppt

the more widespread violence of warlords and militia commanders. This is why a five pillar security sector reform programme was instituted during a donors conference in Geneva, Switzerland in April 2002, with the United States taking the lead role in reforming and reconstructing the Afghan Army, Germany taking the lead on policing, Italy leading judicial reform, the United Kingdom heading counter-narcotics, and Japan leading the demobilization effort.[6]

2.6 The "lead nation" concept for security sector reform, however, has drawbacks in that it allows countries to leave much of the work to those "lead" countries when they themselves may have expertise and other resources to offer. While donor governments are coming to terms with this problem and are expanding their contributions for security sector reform, Afghanistan could benefit from the additional strengthening of ISAF and NATO peace operations. *The United Kingdom should lead the ARRC and ISAF operations in the direction of increased and improved peace operations, especially in accelerating and deepening security sector reform, rather than using resources for combat operations with Operation Enduring Freedom.*

3. THE PITFALLS OF EXPANDING NATO'S MANDATE INTO COMBAT OPERATIONS

3.1 Expanding NATO's efforts into combat operations, whether under or alongside Operation Enduring Freedom, is likely to compromise the peace operations that NATO has invested in ISAF since 2003. *An even stronger peace operations presence and a more robust indigenous security sector are more critical for dealing with what will be a long-term threat to Afghanistan.*

3.2 Of course, the United Kingdom is already fighting alongside other NATO-member countries in Operation Enduring Freedom. The important point is how combat and peace operations are organized and where the United Kingdom's military resources provide the most "value added". Just as important is taking into account the perceptions of Afghans towards troops engaged in combat and peace operations.

3.3 As NATO plans its expansion into Afghanistan's southern, eastern and border regions where insurgents are most active, alliance-led forces will face the prospect of engaging in high levels of combat. Different levels of engagement are possible for NATO. However, a sketch of three scenarios for NATO operations in Afghanistan reveals that merging alliance operations and Operation Enduring Freedom may not be the best way forward for Afghanistan's stabilisation and reconstruction. These three scenarios include:

(a) Merging NATO operations and Operation Enduring Freedom, or keeping operations separate, but with NATO taking on Enduring Freedom-type combat roles;

(b) Having NATO take over the combat operations of Enduring Freedom and handing peace operations over to another international organisation or coalition; or,

(c) Continuing NATO's current focus on peace operations through ISAF and letting Operation Enduring Freedom take care of main combat operations.

3.4 The first two scenarios have NATO visibly engaged in combat on the same level of intensity as Operation Enduring Freedom. The last scenario suggests maintaining NATO's role in ISAF peace operations without taking on Enduring Freedom-type combat responsibilities, and highlights areas that the United Kingdom could improve with its leverage as lead of the ARRC when it takes command of ISAF in May 2006.

(a) *Merge NATO operations and Operation Enduring Freedom or keep operations separate, but with NATO taking on an Enduring Freedom-type combat role*

3.5 According to NATO Spokesman James Appathurai, one option is for NATO to create "'two task forces with separate missions, but brought together near the top under one command' . . . which would require revising the military rules of engagement to allow combat by ISAF." During a meeting at the White House in the summer of 2005, NATO Secretary General Jaap de Hoop Scheffer iterated that these plans were being taken seriously. "One could find a way to have two separate missions", de Hoop Scheffer said, "with a combat mission and a distinct peacekeeping mission under the umbrella of ISAF and a unified NATO command".[7]

3.6 While the exact configurations for NATO involvement in combat operations under or with Operation Enduring Freedom are not entirely clear, merging under one command and having ISAF take on a combat role may seem more efficient in the sense that NATO will enter an environment that has coalition partners that are already members of NATO. If NATO had "two separate missions", it would allow some NATO countries to contribute to peace operations without having to contribute to new combat operations. In

---

[6] US GAO, "Afghanistan Security: Efforts to Establish Army and Police Have Made Progress, but Future Plans Need to be Better Defined", GAO-05-575, 30 June 2005.

[7] Tyson, Ann Scott, "NATO Plans Afghan Presence", *Washington Post*, 2 June 2005, URL http://www.washingtonpost.com/wp-dyn/content/article/2005/06/01/AR2005060101724.html

addition, many see NATO's chance to prove its mettle in the post-cold war and out-of-Europe operations through its mission in Afghanistan. One NATO official has said, "Afghanistan is where NATO's credibility is on the line".[8]

3.7 While NATO expansion into a combat role in southern and eastern Afghanistan and elsewhere as needed may have some of those practical benefits, either of these configurations (whether working under or alongside Operation Enduring Freedom) poses two problems. First, intensifying NATO's responsibility in the country to include full-fledged combat operations will strain NATO's resources for ISAF peace operations. Second, having NATO participate in high-level combat operations could harm ISAF's efforts in peace operations by altering Afghan perceptions towards NATO.

NATO capabilities and resources for combat and peace operations roles in Afghanistan

3.8 If NATO were to take on a combat role, and current US troops (now between 18–20,000 in Operation Enduring Freedom) were to draw down, NATO would need to increase its troop presence to fill the gap and commit troops that would be dedicated to this new combat role in Afghanistan. Although some NATO member countries are serving in Enduring Freedom, separate from ISAF operations, NATO would probably need to significantly bolster its troop numbers and equipment to take on the new mission. *The strain on NATO resources in fulfilling existing ISAF peace operations, together with likely opposition among several major NATO members for a broadening of its mandate, suggest that the alliance would have a difficult time garnering enough resources to take over a new combat mission in addition to sustaining current peace operations.*

3.9 Taking over ISAF in 2003 was a logistical challenge for NATO. Over the course of two years, NATO came under pressure to take over Provincial Reconstruction Teams (PRTs)[9] and expand its presence beyond Kabul. Transport helicopter and troop shortfalls have dogged NATO's Afghan operations,[10] although these problems have since been resolved. NATO reports that ISAF currently conducts patrols in 16 police districts in Kabul and surrounding areas. ISAF has two Regional Area Coordinators, its northern Regional Area Coordinator located in Kunduz and its western one in Herat. These have PRTs underneath them, with five in the northern and four in the western regions.[11] ISAF's area of operation now covers more than 50% of Afghanistan.[12]

3.10 Some alliance members want to expand NATO's investment in Afghanistan's security, but exactly how to make this investment is in dispute. US administration officials sound eager to have NATO take on counter-insurgency operations and UK Defence Secretary John Reid is drawing up plans to put UK forces into the south in a counter-terrorism role. He also wants to lead an initiative to bring all troops in Afghanistan under one command, "I am going to try to bring closer together the US Operation Enduring Freedom, which is aimed at counter-terrorism, and the International Security Assistance Force, which is aimed at other areas",[13]

3.11 French, German, and Spanish officials, as revealed during the most recent meeting of NATO ministers, do not want to have NATO take on the type of combat role reserved for Operation Enduring Freedom and do not want NATO joined with Enduring Freedom under one command (even though Germany has some troops working with the coalition under Operation Enduring Freedom, separate from NATO's ISAF operations).[14] France, which has special forces soldiers working alongside US troops in Afghanistan, has voiced particularly strong opposition to merging the two missions. A French Defence Ministry official said recently, "the two missions were completely different. If you suddenly merge special forces or heavy counter-terrorism units with stabilising forces, which is NATO's role in Afghanistan, then you completely undermine NATO's role".[15]

3.12 The lack of political support from these three key European countries is likely to mean that NATO will have a hard time finding enough troops to take on a new combat role. This is despite some reports that the UK Defence Secretary is planning to announce a large troop increase for Afghanistan—maybe up to

---

[8] Richter, Paul, "NATO Balking at Iraq Mission", *Los Angeles Times*, 9 May 2004.

[9] "A PRT is a combination of international military and civilian personnel based in provincial areas of Afghanistan with the aim of extending the authority of the Afghan central government and helping to facilitate development and reconstruction, primarily by contributing to an improved security environment. PRTs also aim to support Afghan security sector reform—the demobilisation and disarmament of militias; building an accountable army and national police force under democratic control; stamping out the drugs trade; and building a legal system" (Afghanistan Group, FCO, "Afghanistan: Paper on UK PRT Experience", 20 January 2005).

[10] Fiorenza, Nicholas, "NATO Seeks More Troops for ISAF in Afghanistan", *Defense News,* 8 November 2004, p 18.

[11] The United Kingdom has said of the PRTs under its charge, that they "focus primarily on reconstruction and have limited roles in providing direct security for local Afghans and in working with Afghan army and police" (US GAO, "Afghanistan Security", *OpCit*).

[12] "History of the International Security Assistance Force", NATO website, updated 14 September 2005.

[13] Sinclair, Paul, "More Troops on the Way to Take on the Taliban: Reid Set to Send 4000 to Kabul", *Daily Record,* 1 October 2005.

[14] "UK Backs Afghan Troop Expansion", BBC News, 1 October 2005.

[15] Dempsey, Judy and Cloud, David S, "Europeans Balking at New Afghan Role, *International Herald Tribune*, 14 September 2005, p 1.

4,000—in addition to the 900 UK troops currently in Afghanistan.[16] At the time of writing this submission, it was unclear whether these troops would be earmarked for coalition combat operations or for NATO peace operations. Germany, which still opposes the idea of placing ISAF under command of Operation Enduring Freedom, is also moving in the direction of increasing its troop strength in the country by adding 750 troops to its current deployment of 2,250.[17] However, Germany's contribution would be for ISAF peace operations only.[18]

3.13 *If NATO becomes overwhelmed by a new combat role and no other organisation can fill the ISAF role, Afghanistan could be left without a peace operations plan and the country would fall victim to the same problems it has experienced in years past.* Moreover, without strong peace operations, the combat role will become all the more difficult because more Afghans might become inclined to join groups opposed to Western intervention, especially if the conditions that created the various warring factions in the first place are allowed to fester and grow once more.

How a new combat role for NATO could change Afghan perceptions towards ISAF peace operations

3.14 Increasing the alienation of Afghans from ISAF peace operations could also refuel insurgencies. In addition to becoming wary of foreign combat operations overall, for ISAF to work in both peace operations and combat operations, with Operation Enduring Freedom it could jeopardise any trust that ISAF members have built with local Afghans.

3.15 To argue that NATO should not take on an Enduring Freedom-type role is not to say that the alliance currently has an indifferent peacekeeping role. ISAF is not a traditional peacekeeping operation in the sense of being an impartial broker among various competing groups. ISAF has some of the same contributing countries that coalition forces have in Operation Enduring Freedom and these countries oppose the influence of Al Qaeda and Taliban ideologies. The roles demanded by Operation Enduring Freedom, however, would require a much more combat-driven and hostile presence that would not mix well with the image that ISAF personnel, whether military or civilian, want to project toward Afghans.

3.16 First, *decision makers need to remember that the roles of combat and peace operations troops are distinctive.* The PRT concept itself came from the military-civil-affairs (CA) units. According to one analyst, "CA units differ from regular military forces in that they are designed and trained to facilitate civil-governance functions and public sector services, as opposed to troops and units that are equipped and trained to conduct combat operations".[19] Some PRTs, however, have served as bases for small counter-insurgency operations and this has put into question the viability of PRTs for peace operations. Overall, although NATO troops have gone through combat training at one point at least in their careers, their roles have become specialised through ISAF peace operations.[20]

3.17 A well-known precept in peace operations and one that is stated in US Army field manuals declares, "Every soldier must be aware that the goal is to produce conditions that are conducive to peace and not to the destruction of an enemy. The enemy is the conflict."[21] The manual goes on to argue that diplomatic considerations take priority over purely military requirements and constraints on the use of force are important to building better relations with civilians. On the other hand, NATO troops sent into counter-insurgency missions in Afghanistan will develop an entirely different relationship (if much of one at all) with locals.

3.18 Second, *decision makers also need to keep in mind that a closer identification of peace and combat operations could harm ISAF efforts.* Lt Col Donna Boltz said it well in her research on the role of peace operations:

> The measure of success is not dominating the enemy but influencing the affected parties to create the conditions for a stable environment in which businesses flourish, children regularly attend schools, and families live free from the fear of being forced from their homes. It is clear, then, that a relationship of trust and understanding must exist between and among the military, police, and civilians supporting the operation as well as members of the threatened, failing, or failed state.[22]

---

[16] "No Troop Withdrawal Yet—Reid", *icCroydon*, 1 October 2005 and "UK Backs Afghan Troop Expansion", BBC News, 1 October 2005.

[17] Nicola, Stefan, "Germany Extends Afghanistan Mandate", *International Relations and Security Network* 30 September 2005.

[18] Williamson, Hugh, *Financial Times* via *Yahoo! News*, 29 September 2005.

[19] Borders, Robert, "Provincial Reconstruction Teams in Afghanistan: A Model for Post-Conflict Reconstruction and Development", *Journal of Development and Social Transformation*, Volume 1, November 2004, p 7.

[20] Borders explains, "While military civil affairs units are comprised of soldiers, they are not combat troops in the traditional sense, nor are they trained as such. They have a unique skill set, or Military Occupational Specialty, designed to provide commanders in the field with resident technical capability and expertise on all matters related to civil affairs" (Borders, Robert, "Provincial Reconstruction", *OpCit*, p 8).

[21] Headquarters, Department of the US Army, *Peace Operations: Field Manual 100–23*, 30 December 1994, as shown in "Information Operations: IO in A Peace Enforcement Environment", Newsletter No 99–2, February 1999, via GlobalSecurity.org.

[22] Lt Col Boltz, Donna G, "Information Technology and Peace Support Operations: Relationship for the New Millennium" *Virtual Diplomacy*, United States Institute of Peace, 22 July 2002.

3.19 For NATO to take on counter-insurgency operations and continue peace operations will require some alliance troops to "dominate the enemy", while other troops will need to develop more trusting relationships with Afghans. This mixing of roles for NATO could confuse Afghan civilians and place NATO troops in more precarious and ambiguous situations.

3.20 Already, some analysts are arguing that combat and peace operations have influenced one another too much. A report from the UN Joint Logistics Centre argues, "Both forces [from ISAF and Operation Enduring Freedom] are in uniform and are, irrespective of their functions/affiliations/mandates, indistinguishable to the public, with the image portrayed by one, inevitably influencing the acceptance of the other".[23] Whether or not this assessment exaggerates the current perceptions of connections between peace operations and combat troops, having NATO take over combat missions in addition to its current peace operations will only exacerbate this problem.

3.21 Moreover, *expanding ISAF in an Enduring Freedom-type operation could worsen already tense relations between PRTs and non-governmental humanitarian organisations*. Humanitarian principles hold that aid should be provided in an impartial and apolitical basis. Many NGOs on the ground have concerns about the way PRTs are managed, partly because military organisations have been perceived as infringing on NGO space.[24] Cassandra Nelson, a senior spokeswoman for Mercy Corps-Afghanistan, summarised the point: "When we tackle reconstruction, we don't have the stigma of having carried guns".[25] Yet the PRTs often operate where NGOs cannot because those environs have been too dangerous.[26]

3.22 Finally, were NATO to merge its operations with Enduring Freedom it would have international legal implications. Currently, ISAF has a UN-approved mandate.[27] Should policymakers try to merge ISAF with Enduring Freedom's mission, ISAF could lose its UN-approved mandate if enough countries were to oppose the adoption of an additional counter-insurgency/combat role.

(b) *Allow NATO to take over the combat duties similar to Operation Enduring Freedom and have a different organisation take over peace support operations.*

3.23 In October 2005, NATO's Secretary-General Jaap de Hoop Scheffer said in an interview with *US News and World Report* that he "would like to see NATO take the lead in all of Afghanistan".[28] The Secretary-General said in the same interview that he does not believe the United States and the rest of NATO should merge Operation Enduring Freedom and ISAF operations.[29] Whether or not it was intended, the statement raises the possibility of Operation Enduring Freedom coming to a close, at least in its current form, and NATO taking over combat operations, mainly against Al Qaeda and Taliban insurgents in southern and eastern Afghanistan. Another organisation, or a coalition of the willing, would need to pick up peace operations from NATO.

3.24 Having NATO take over Operation Enduring Freedom and abandon its peace operations duties would permit the continued separation of organisations overseeing different missions. Moreover, the problem in the first scenario could be avoided for NATO because the alliance could transfer and focus all of its resources in Afghanistan on the combat mission.

3.25 Leaving peace operations for other organisations or a coalition of the willing, however, could leave Afghanistan without the peace operations assistance that it still requires. Right now, no other organisation has the same capacity for peace operations in Afghanistan as NATO.

3.26 The EU and United Nations are the only two organisations that could be considered for the magnitude of ISAF operations in Afghanistan, but both lack the resources to take on the entire challenge. (Certainly, other organisations, such as the OSCE, have contributed to facets of Afghanistan's reconstruction, such as election monitoring.) The EU has been developing its capabilities to conduct the so-called Petersberg Tasks,[30] which include undertaking high-intensity peace operations. The EU has also been ramping up its policing and civilian crisis management capabilities. The EU has tested its emerging capacities in Africa and in the Former Yugoslav Republic of Macedonia. But while the EU has already made some contributions to Afghanistan's reconstruction, it does not have anything like enough personnel ready for conducting the kind of large-scale missions that an Afghanistan-type operation would require. Similarly,

[23] UN Joint Logistics Centre, "Civil-Military Collaboration in Afghanistan", last updated 10 March, 2005.
[24] Borders, Robert, "Provincial Reconstruction", *OpCit*, p 5.
[25] *Ibid* p 7.
[26] NGO workers have been the target of Taliban and Al Qaeda-related attacks, but it is unclear whether these attacks occur because these groups are often comprised of foreigners or as a result of suspicions of NGO collaboration with military troops. When troops were donning civilian clothes (a practice which has since been stopped), insurgents may have come to the conclusion that there was no distinction between NGO humanitarian workers and soldiers, which could have made NGO personnel more vulnerable (Borders, Robert, 2 Provincial Reconstruction", *OpCit*, pp 7–8).
[27] ISAF has been deployed under the UN authorisation of Security Council Resolutions 1386, 1413, and 1444 as a peace enforcement mission and to assist in the maintenance of security so as to help the Afghan Transitional Authority (NATO, International Security Assistance Force, Frequently Asked Questions, 23 May 2005).
[28] "The NATO Perspective," *US News & World Report*, 3 October 2005.
[29] *Ibid*.
[30] The Petersberg Tasks include peacekeeping, combat tasks related to crisis management, and humanitarian and rescue work.

while the United Nations has participated in Afghanistan's reconstruction process, it suffers from under-funding and a lack of consensus and confidence, and is unlikely to be able to pull together the personnel and other resources necessary to deploy the kind of peace operation that could completely take over the work of ISAF.

3.27 Whereas no other organisation has NATO's capacity for undertaking peace operations in Afghanistan, it is a job that NATO cannot do alone. The peace operation is crucially reliant on the contributions of other international organisations. For example, NATO is not equipped to undertake all of the civil functions necessary for a successful reconstruction of the security sector, and the alliance needs organisations such as the EU with its experience in the Balkans reconstruction process.[31]

3.28 Therefore, *NATO should deepen and extend its relationships with other international organisations in Afghanistan because these relationships will improve the overall effectiveness of Afghanistan's reconstruction process. In the longer-term, the alliance should consider handing over peace operations (including reconstruction) to non-military organisations, especially as levels of violence hopefully decrease.* A UN report warns what could happen if NATO runs peace operations for too long in Afghanistan:

> The challenge of policymakers is to recognise that there is a distinction between the three endeavours of warfare, reconstruction, and occupation. Coalition forces and NATO/ISAF forces are trained to prevail in the first; they can be helpful in the second under certain conditions; but if they undertake the reconstruction in a highly visible manner over an extended period of time, and combined reconstruction with information gathering and other unrelated pseudo-military activities, they will be perceived by the public as an occupying force . . . If they raise expectations that they can "get the job done" and later fail to "deliver the goods", the self-inflicted damage extends worldwide and far into the future.[32]

3.28 In the short-term, however, *NATO is necessary to the success of peace operations in Afghanistan. NATO and other contributing countries should seek to strengthen and improve current peace operations, rather than move into combat roles.*

(c) *Continue current NATO ISAF mission, but with improvements*

3.29 Continuing the current ISAF mission along current lines is not the ideal way to proceed, although it may be less harmful than if NATO were to take on Operation Enduring Freedom's tasks. *Rather than becoming burdened with a larger combat mission, the United Kingdom should seek to improve peace operations in Afghanistan by encouraging (a) other donor countries to do more in security sector reform and (b) other international organisations beyond NATO (such as the EU, OSCE and UN agencies) to become more involved.* NATO may need to focus more on force protection in the south and east and the alliance may need to take its time with this expansion, but it should not engage in the type of combat and counter-insurgency operations undertaken by Operation Enduring Freedom.

3.30 While NATO's ISAF operations have had a limited role in rebuilding Afghanistan's security sector, this is a facet of the country's reconstruction where NATO could have a major legitimate and effective impact. NATO will need to insure that Afghan nationals are brought into running these processes as much as possible so a sense of ownership takes hold and Afghans can sustain these programs after contributing countries depart.

Training of the Afghan National Army

3.31 Coalition countries, mainly under the leadership of the United States, with assistance from Bulgaria, Canada, France, Germany, Mongolia, Romania, South Korea, and the United Kingdom have provided military trainers for the Afghan army.[33] They have trained about 28,000 local troops, with a goal of fielding 70,000 troops by 2007.[34] However, the development of core military institutions that will hold the Afghan National Army (ANA) together, such as logistics commands, is lagging behind the basic training of troops.[35] Without the creation of strong military institutions, Afghan troops will lack a solid basis for guidance and the ANA will not have a sense of cohesion that can build loyalty and discipline. The army could become fractured and more susceptible to infiltration by insurgent groups.

3.32 With a considerable number of troops left to train and a special need to develop core military institutions, NATO could take on a more specialised role in this aspect of Afghanistan's security sector reform. NATO has been training Iraqi officers, and has years of experience with training its own officers and those of future alliance members. If the United States is eager to draw down some of its troops in

---

[31] Dobbins, James, "NATO Peacekeepers Need a Partner", *International Herald Tribune*, 20 September 2005.

[32] UN Joint Logistics Centre, "Civil-Military Collaboration in Afghanistan", last updated 10 March, 2005.

[33] These targets for troop strength and ANA reconstruction have been stated US goals (US GAO, "Afghanistan Security", *OpCit.*).

[34] O'Hanlon, Michael and Kamp, Nina, "Afghanistan Index", *OpCit.*

[35] US GAO, "Afghanistan Security", *OpCit.*

Afghanistan, it would make more sense for NATO to continue building upon its peace operations role and training expertise, rather than devoting its resources to a full-fledged combat role that could endanger its peace operations.

Disarmament and Demobilisation

3.33 ISAF has worked with Afghanistan's government and the United Nations in support of the disarmament, demobilisation, and reintegration of former combatants. According to ISAF's website, it will work as part of a new programme that will disarm an estimated 120,000 illegal armed men and return them to civilian life.

3.34 Despite ISAF and Japan's work in Afghan disarmament, an NGO researcher recently found some local commanders and units re-arming at a rate of 2–20%.[36] One commander has over 12,000 light weapons and is trafficking them in order to replace the income that he lost through disarmament.[37] As mentioned above, the disarmament of warlords and militia has been a top concern for Afghans. Unfortunately, after the end of Soviet occupation and Afghanistan's civil war, it was the Taliban who disarmed the warlords. Thus, disarmament plays a symbolic as well as a practical security role in Afghanistan.

3.35 With NATO's experience in weapons collection and destruction in the Balkans, for example, *the alliance should continue and intensify its role in disarmament*. As Afghanistan's security sector is reconstructed, NATO should train Afghans in disarmament procedures to insure that legitimate indigenous forces have the ability to carry out these tasks independent of foreign assistance in the future.

Other needs in security sector reform

3.36 While the training of police is not necessarily the type of role NATO has taken on in the past, *the need for a more effective police force in Afghanistan is so urgent that the UK government, through NATO and any other channels, needs to bring more resources to bear on police reform*. While Afghan army troops have performed relatively well according to some anecdotal evidence, the national police have had a far more difficult time. According to US State and Defense Department accounts, "many of the untrained officers remain loyal to local militias in an environment dominated by ethnic loyalties. Working with untrained colleagues, newly trained policemen often find it difficult to apply the principles they learned during training".[38]

3.37 There are estimated to be about 50,000 men working as police in Afghanistan, but they are "generally untrained, poorly equipped, illiterate (70–90%), and often owe their allegiance to local warlords and militia commanders rather than the central government".[39] Many of those serving as police are former Mujahedeen who have experienced a lifetime of combat and are "accustomed to acting with impunity".[40] The Afghan National Police (ANP) has over 35,000 members trained, but the goal is to have 62,000.[41] While Germany has taken the lead in police training, the United States also started to train Afghan police, but with a shortened method that does not include weapons or literacy training.[42]

3.38 *Organisations such as the EU and OSCE have proven track records in police training in other countries. Broader participation from these two organisations in Afghanistan is essential*. The UK government has donated about £1 million to police reconstruction in Afghanistan (as of January 2005[43]) and the United Kingdom is generally becoming more involved in police reform through the PRTs.[44] As of January 2005, the EU has donated about £48 million to the reconstruction of the Afghan National Police, while (as of June 2005) the United States had contributed about £486 million.[45] Germany, the lead nation for police reconstruction, had spent £38 million (as of January 2005[46]), mostly on police reconstruction in Kabul.[47]

3.39 All of this funding on police and security sector reform is welcome, but Afghanistan will need more resources, both financial and human, from international organisations and country donors for this undertaking to be a success. For instance, peace operations in East Timor, Bosnia and Kosovo benefited from field-based training and mentoring. Currently, however, US officials are saying that deploying such trainers throughout Afghanistan and into dangerous areas is too expensive. *The first-year cost to implement a countrywide field-based training and mentoring programme in Afghanistan has been estimated at £90*

---

[36] Dennys, Christian, "Disarmament, Demobilisation and Rearmament: The Effects of Disarmament in Afghanistan", *Japan Afghan NGO Network Occasional Paper*, 6 June 2005, p 7.

[37] *Ibid.*

[38] US GAO, "Afghanistan Security", *OpCit.*

[39] Miller, Laurel and Perito, Robert, "Establishing the Rule of Law in Afghanistan", *United States Institute of Peace Special Report* 117, March 2004.

[40] *Ibid.*

[41] US GAO, "Afghanistan Security", *OpCit.*

[42] Terakhelis, Shahabuddin, "Reforming Police Will Take Time", IWPR, e-Ariana, 7 June 2004.

[43] US GAO, "Afghanistan Security", *OpCit.*

[44] Afghanistan Group, FCO, "Afghanistan: Paper on UK PRT Experience", 20 January 2005.

[45] US GAO, "Afghanistan Security", *OpCit.*

[46] *Ibid.*

[47] Miller, Laurel and Perito, Robert, "Establishing the Rule of Law in Afghanistan", *OpCit.*

million.[48] ***The UK government should take the lead in fundraising for and developing such a programme.*** Another option, beyond current joint patrolling between ISAF and Kabul police, is for NATO troops to guard police trainers supplied by the EU or the OSCE as part of a field-based training program.

3.40 Other areas of security sector reform, such as judicial restructuring and the rule of law, largely fall outside NATO's remit. Of course, military and police reforms will not be as effective without a functioning justice system and fair penal institutions. The rule of law is important at all levels of Afghan society. Where the law is not enforced, Afghans are likely to turn towards warlords, tribal chiefs, or whoever else can provide security. This will often be those who have the weapons and who already hold power at the local level, such as the Taliban.[49]

4. CONCLUSION

4.1 A country that has endured 30 years of civil war and was a key breeding ground for Al Qaeda terrorists is not going to be turned around overnight. Much has been achieved in four years of coalition anti-terrorism operations and a shorter period of ISAF peace operations, but much more remains to be done. Afghanistan is still a long way from being able to survive without outside help. Many more years of engagement by the international community will be required before the country can be expected to run an effective government throughout its territory, and even then it will need foreign aid and investment for years to come.

4.2 It is in the UK government and NATO's interest, and most importantly in the interest of Afghans, for peace operations in Afghanistan to succeed. This is more likely to happen if NATO remains focused on these operations instead of taking on a full-fledged combat and counter-insurgency programme.

7 October 2005

Memorandum from the Ministry of Defence

BRITISH MILITARY OPERATIONS IN AFGHANISTAN

INTRODUCTION

1. The UK remains committed to the emergence of a prosperous, democratic, secure and stable Afghanistan. The UK government effort is especially focussed on counter narcotics, security sector reform and developing a sustainable economy based on legitimate activity. Good progress has been made in terms of stabilising the overall security situation, building the capacity of Afghan security forces and extending the authority of the Government of Afghanistan across the country. The National Assembly and Provincial Council elections held on 18 September represented a major step forward in Afghanistan's development as a fledgling democratic state. There remain, however, considerable challenges ahead: the extension of the NATO led International Security Assistance Force (ISAF) into the south and east of Afghanistan; achieving greater synergy between the NATO and Coalition missions, leading in time to a NATO Mission across the whole of Afghanistan; the continuing development of Afghan security forces; dealing with the opium trade and how to build on and consolidate the success of the Bonn Process with a new framework for the future. Afghanistan has been NATO's principal operational priority since it assumed control of ISAF in 2003. The deployment to Kabul of the HQ ARRC Group, to lead ISAF from May 2006, will make a major contribution to these efforts at the same time as the UK moves the focus of its military effort from the north to the south of the country. But this military deployment alone will not guarantee success. An integrated approach covering security, governance, development and counter-narcotics is vital. There is a virtuous circle where increased security supports development which in turn improves security. Development and reconstruction are key to our success—crucial because without them, military intervention would not necessarily increase stability and security.

SECURITY SITUATION

2. The security situation in Afghanistan is broadly stable, if fragile, with levels of violence driven by a range of factors including tribal rivalry, criminal activity and seasonal factors including the weather. There was an upsurge in violence preceding the 18 September National Assembly elections, as widely anticipated, though polling day was not significantly disrupted. Neither insurgent groups nor the range of illegally armed groups (IAGs) currently pose a credible strategic threat to the stability of Afghanistan.

3. The International Military Presence in Afghanistan, comprising the NATO-led ISAF and the US-led Coalition, is designed to:

— Prevent Afghanistan reverting to ungoverned space which could harbour terrorism.

---

[48] US GAO, "Afghanistan Security", *OpCit.*
[49] CSIS, "In the Balance: Measuring Progress in Afghanistan", July 2005.

— Build security and government institutions so that the progress of recent years becomes irreversible, and to enable eventual international military disengagement.

— Support efforts to counter the growth of narcotics production and trafficking.

ISAF AND THE COALITION

4. ISAF came into being at the end of 2001, and has operated under NATO command since 11 August 2003. ISAF is present in Afghanistan at the request of the Afghan government, and under the authorisation of successive United Nations Security Council Resolutions. The latest (UNSCR 1623) was agreed on 13 September 2005. Since October 2003, when the UN Security Council agreed to extend the mandate of ISAF beyond Kabul, NATO forces have extended into the north and west of Afghanistan and are now looking to expand into the south, increasing security and stability and extending the authority of the Government of Afghanistan across the whole of Afghanistan. Having made this commitment to Afghanistan, NATO Allies will now need to demonstrate the will and resolve, and allocate the necessary resources, to make a success of this engagement. The long-term aim for the Alliance must be to consolidate the gains made so far and build indigenous Afghan capacity, so that international military forces can eventually disengage from Afghanistan.

5. Coalition forces are commanded by Combined Forces Command-Afghanistan (CFC-A), with its US-led headquarters in Kabul, which in turn comes under US Central Command (CENTCOM) in Tampa, Florida. The UK provides the Deputy Commanding General for CFC-A. CFC-A currently has some 18,000 personnel under command. The US also has the G8 lead for developing the Afghan National Army, currently some 28,000 strong.

THE PROVINCIAL RECONSTRUCTION TEAM (PRT) CONCEPT

6. ISAF operates primarily through Provincial Reconstruction Teams (PRTs): joint civil-military teams deployed to extend the influence of the Government of Afghanistan beyond Kabul, facilitating the development of Security Sector Reform (SSR) and the reconstruction effort, and thereby helping create the conditions for a stable and secure environment. Each PRT is configured and operated according to the prevailing security situation, socio-economic conditions and terrain in the region they are operating. All ISAF PRTs work to NATO's Operational Plan (OPLAN 10302), which sets the framework for ISAF to conduct military operations across Afghanistan, in co-operation with indigenous and coalition forces. PRTs seek to achieve their objectives through dialogue and liaison with all actors operating in the region. This includes local military, political and religious leaders, Afghan Government representatives, UNAMA and Coalition partners. PRTs generally maintain a light footprint and are not designed to impose security on the region, but rather to help the Afghan people create a safe and stable environment themselves.

7. The UK PRT comprises representatives of the armed forces, as well as from DFID and the FCO, representatives from other nations and a security sector expert from the Afghan government. The Afghan representative allows the PRT to demonstrate that it is a joint international/Afghan operation; and it allows the PRT to draw on Afghan experience of dealing with the local population and officials. The UK PRT works extremely closely with the local UNAMA Regional Office. It has successfully supported local disarmament initiatives, brokered by UNAMA, by lobbying local factional leaders to engage constructively in the process, and by monitoring their compliance. The UK PRT is increasingly becoming involved in police reform and remains closely involved in supporting the 300 Afghan national policemen deployed from Kabul to Mazar-e Sharif in October 2003 to overcome the factional nature of the existing force. The UK funds five UK police advisers/mentors to work alongside US colleagues at the Regional Police Training College in Mazar. This has led to particularly close liaison between the PRTs, the FCO, DFID and police advisers, focused on effective deployment of trained recruits across the region. ANA and local police elements now routinely conduct joint patrols in the region. There is clear evidence to suggest that this action has reduced levels of banditry in previously notorious areas. It has also won the support of the local population, which clearly appreciates the effective presence of indigenous, centralised security institutions.

NATO'S MISSION IN AFGHANISTAN

8. The international military presence in Afghanistan will have most effect if ISAF and Coalition forces can initially be drawn into greater synergy and, ultimately, NATO taking responsibility for the main military effort in Afghanistan. This will:

— Eliminate ISAF/Coalition duplication of effort and provide clearer command and control.

— Provide a single international military entity with which the Afghan authorities can engage.

— Take full advantage of HQ ARRC's presence in 2006–07.

— Provide—with HQ ARRC deployment and ISAF expansion—a push towards long-term stabilisation of the Afghan security situation, and ultimate ownership of Afghan security by the Afghans themselves, at a crucial point in the country's development.

— Present a single international community front to those (including the illegally armed groups and Taliban) who continue to oppose the development of Afghanistan.

— Provide impetus for NATO to continue its evolution towards becoming a more operationally effective organisation.

A NATO-led mission across Afghanistan can only be achieved once ISAF expansion is complete. The UK is therefore working to support and facilitate the expansion of ISAF into the south (see below) as the next stage in the process. It is important to stress that a NATO-led mission would be concerned with the existing ISAF tasks—reconstruction and counter-insurgency (COIN). Counter-terrorism (in the sense of targeted operations against known terrorist groups), would remain the responsibility of residual specialist Coalition force elements operating alongside NATO. The mechanisms for increased alignment of the two missions, including the detailed command and control arrangements, are still being discussed.

CURRENT UK DEPLOYMENTS

9. The UK led the first ISAF deployment to Kabul in 2001. The current UK commitment to ISAF comprises a PRT in the north of Afghanistan (Mazar-e-Sharif), the Forward Support Base and Quick Reaction Force for Area North, an infantry company that serves as the Kabul Patrol Company (KPC) in Kabul, and staff officers in HQ ISAF. UK staff officers, a training team for the Afghan National Army and a detachment of six Harrier GR7 aircraft serve with the Coalition (the Harriers provide Close Air Support (CAS) and air reconnaissance to both ISAF and the Coalition). We handed over our responsibility for the PRT in Maymaneh to the Norwegians on 1 September 2005.

FUTURE UK DEPLOYMENTS

10. The Prime Minister announced the intention to deploy the HQ ARRC Group to Afghanistan at the NATO ministerial meeting in Istanbul in July 2004. The UK believes that, with the deployment of the ARRC for a nine month period from May next year, (back-to-back with the Italians who took over ISAF leadership in August 2005), there is an opportunity for a "step change" in the international commitment to Afghanistan. The UK government has been considering further deployments to Afghanistan in this strategic context. As the Secretary of State made clear in a media briefing on 13 September, from next April we plan to move our forces from the North of Afghanistan to a base in Helmand province in the South. We shall establish a new British-led Provincial Reconstruction Team at Lashkar Gah. But the Taliban are still active in the area. So are drugs traffickers. The overall operating environment is therefore less benign than in other parts of ISAF's current area of operation. We must be prepared to support, even defend, the Provincial Reconstruction Team. That means that, with Allies, we shall need a stronger military presence in the south than is currently required for the PRTs operating in the North.

11. We are discussing with NATO what those additional forces should be. We are currently engaged with the NATO force generation process, which will determine the detail of UK and Allied contributions to ISAF expansion in the south. Once the UK has determined an appropriate force package, a full statement to Parliament will be made about the UK commitment.

12. In addition to the strategic effect of this deployment in terms of enabling ISAF expansion, the UK has chosen to focus its efforts on Helmand Province because we believe we can make a difference in supporting the counter-narcotics effort and in countering the continuing threat to stability from the residual Taliban insurgency, illegally armed groups and criminal activity. The province is in the heartland of the narcotics trade, with more opium poppy cultivated there annually than in any other region in Afghanistan. We also plan to build Afghan National Army and Police capacity with a view to transferring responsibility for security in the medium term. The military deployment will be closely linked with political engagement and development efforts in the province.

SECURITY SECTOR REFORM

13. The military effort is just one element of the international effort in Afghanistan. The key point for wider engagement in Afghanistan is that the deployment of military resources alone does not provide the long term solution. The keys to sustainable reconstruction are wide international engagement and, in a national context, the involvement of several elements of the Whitehall machine. Building the capacity of the Afghan authorities is one essential part of this international development. The Bonn process set the initial agenda for the security sector reform process and there remains work ongoing in each of the G8 lead areas: police reform, judicial reform, Disarmament, Demobilisation and Reintegration (DDR), building the Afghan National Army (ANA) and Counter-Narcotics. Developing an effective ANA will be crucial to achieving future stability in Afghanistan. The UK has provided funding to support the ANA and is involved in training Non-Commissioned Officers. Already the ANA is regularly contributing to operations across Afghanistan. The Disarmament, Demobilisation and Reintegration (DDR) process has gone well with over 60,000 personnel disarmed and over 9,000 heavy weapons cantoned. The focus is now turning to the more challenging disbandment of illegally armed groups. Progress on police work is ongoing, as is the development of the judicial system, albeit at a slower pace.

14. As the international community re-assesses its engagement in Afghanistan in the post-Bonn period, NATO is currently looking at its future role and how an increased focus on security sector reform can be integrated into ISAF expansion. The UK is encouraging an increased role for NATO in the future, for example building the capacity of the ANA through operational mentoring. There is also scope for increased participation in other activities such as support to the Afghan National Police, support to DDR and more consistent support to the counter narcotics effort, within the scope of the counter-narcotics annex to the NATO OPLAN.

15. On a national level the UK has entered into an "Enduring Relationship" with Afghanistan, signed by the Prime Minister and President Karzai in August, to take forward national assistance in a number of these areas, as part of a wider programme of bilateral assistance.

COUNTER-NARCOTICS

16. It is no longer terrorism, but the cultivation, processing and distribution of opium products that is the greatest threat to Afghan security. The narcotics trade influences senior levels in the government and effectively controls some of the provincial administrations. Counter-Narcotics policy and management of operations is the responsibility of the Afghan authorities—the Ministry for Counter-Narcotics and the Ministry of the Interior. As the G8 lead nation on coordinating international support on counter-narcotics, the UK is committed to eliminating the opium industry, which is seen as central to achieving our long term goals of bringing stability to the country. Military support to counter-narcotics needs to be part of a wider integrated strategy firmly rooted in addressing the issue of alternative livelihoods and the development of a criminal justice system. To this effect, all UK work on counter-narcotics is co-ordinated through the Afghan Drugs Inter-departmental Unit (ADIDU) drawn from the FCO, DFID, MOD, Home Office and HMR&C. The United Nations Office for Drugs and Crime report states that there has been a 21% drop in poppy cultivation this year, down from 131,000 hectares to 103,000 hectares. Overall production was only slightly down however, as favourable weather conditions resulted in an increase in the opium yield per acre from 32 kilogrammes in 2004 to 39 kilogrammes in 2005. But we recognise that this is a significant challenge; there is much to do before Afghanistan is free of this industry and its influence.

Second memorandum from the Ministry of Defence

The attitude of the people towards the International military presence inside Afghanistan

****50

The command and control relationship between the ISAF and OEF missions

1. Command and Control (C2) in Afghanistan is currently exercised by two separate Headquarters (HQs), one for ISAF operations in the North and West and the other for US-led Operation Enduring Freedom (OEF) (which covers the South and East, and all Counter-Terrorism (CT) operations). Coordination and deconfliction of operations is ensured by the placement of liaison officers from each HQ in the other. Once NATO forces are fully in place in the South (Stage 3 area), C2 for that geographical area will transfer to HQ ISAF. The next step, in accordance with the agreed NATO operational plan, would be for the East (Stage 4) to be transferred to ISAF C2, at which point the whole of Afghanistan will be under NATO command for all operations except CT, no decision on Stage 4 has however been taken.

2. The detailed C2 organisation once both Stages 3 and 4 are complete remains to be finalised, although the broad principles have been agreed. The single NATO HQ in Afghanistan will command all ISAF forces conducting security and stabilisation operations. It is likely that the Commander will have two or three deputies, one of whom will be a US officer who will be "double-hatted" with responsibilities for US-led Counter-Terrorism (CT) operations in Afghanistan in addition to his ISAF role; he would be responsible to USCENTCOM for CT operations, since CT is not part of the ISAF mission. This C2 arrangement will clearly offer advantages in terms of coordination and deconfliction, not least through the collocation of commanders and staff working on each type of operation.

3. In terms of C2 for fixed-wing air support, the arrangements post Stage 3 and 4 expansion will accord with well-established principles and doctrine for Air C2, which are designed to ensure that the inherent responsiveness, flexibility and range of air power is utilised to best effect. HQ ISAF's air department will prioritise and designate the tasking for ISAF aircraft. To ensure the safe deconfliction and coordination of all air operations over Afghanistan (including any supporting CT operations), this tasking and the overall airspace plan will be issued from the regional Combined Air Operations Centre (CAOC) in Qatar, which will contain an embedded team from HQ ISAF. A further benefit of using the CAOC for coordination is

---

[50] Asterisks in the memorandum denote that part of the document has not been reported, at the request of the MoD and with the agreement of the Committee.

that, since it has responsibilities for air operations across the wider region (including air operations in Iraq), it has the ability to reprioritise the allocation of long-range aircraft to provide additional support from non-ISAF aircraft to high-priority ISAF operations should that be required. Clearly, air support for the protection of friendly forces on the ground would always be a top priority mission; aircraft will be diverted from other tasks to assist "troops in contact" when required and other aircraft will also be held on short-notice "ground alert" for such missions.

Clarification of the UK's policies and responsibilities towards people arrested during military operations. In particular whether people detained by ISAF forces have been, and will be in future, handed over to US control

4. The legal authority for troops deployed under the ISAF to arrest and detain derives from a series of United Nations Security Council Resolutions, most recently UNSCR 1623 (2005), and by agreement with the Government of Afghanistan. These contain authorisations permitting use of all necessary measures to fulfil the ISAF's mission. ISAF policy, agreed by NATO, is that individuals should be transferred to the Afghan authorities at the first opportunity and within 96 hours, or released. Counter-terrorism is not an ISAF task.

5. NATO Rules of Engagement set out the circumstances in which individuals may be detained by ISAF troops, but do not cover their subsequent handling. As has been the policy of successive governments, we are unable to comment further on the Rules of Engagement under which our forces or those of other NATO Allies deploy, as this may compromise the safety of our troops.

6. Work continues within NATO on clarification of detention issues, in discussion with the Afghan government, as NATO prepares for expansion beyond the North and West of Afghanistan. Handling of detainees after detention is a matter for individual states to negotiate with the Afghan Government as appropriate.

7. Since 2001 we have detained in Afghanistan on very few occasions, and all individuals were subsequently released. The UK has not transferred any detainee to the Afghan authorities or into the custody of US forces, and there are currently no individuals being detained under UK authority in Afghanistan. Current UK policy is not to detain individuals unless absolutely necessary; and indeed it has rarely been necessary to do so in ISAF's current area of operation.

8. Nevertheless, we recognise the possibility that, as we expand ISAF into the more challenging security environment in the south, British troops may more often be exposed to situations in which it becomes necessary temporarily to detain individuals. In such cases the NATO agreed policy of releasing or handing over suspects in as short a time as possible and within 96 hours to the Afghan authorities will still apply. The UK is currently discussing arrangements with the Government of Afghanistan which will cover the possible future transfer of any individual to the Afghan Authorities following detention by UK forces.

9. As the Committee is aware, we have deployed troops to prepare the ground for the future UK deployment to Helmand Province. They are under Coalition rather than ISAF command but should the need arise for them to arrest and detain an individual the same UK principles and guidelines on prisoner handling would apply to them as apply to British troops deployed under the ISAF.

The structure and funding of the Afghan Drugs Inter-Departmental Unit

10. As the lead G8 nation, the UK is co-ordinating international efforts to assist the Government of Afghanistan (GoA) to tackle the counter narcotics (CN) trade. Essential to this is the delivery of the GoA's updated National Drugs Control Strategy (NDCS), which was officially launched at the London Conference on Afghanistan (31 January–1 February). The NCDS sets out the GoA's CN policies over the next three years and highlights four key priorities where activity is likely to make the greatest impact in the short-term, namely:

— Targeting the trafficker and the trade.

— Strengthening and diversifing legal rural livelihoods.

— Developing effective CN institutions.

— Demand reduction.

11. The Afghan Drug Inter-Departmental Unit (ADIDU), based in the UK, and the British Embassy Drugs Team (BEDT) based in Afghanistan, were set up to co-ordinate our activity. Reporting monthly to the Prime Minister, they work closely with law enforcement and intelligence agencies to deliver progress against the NDCS. ADIDU and BEDT include staff from other government departments, including HM Revenue and Customs, Department for International Development, the Home Office, and the Ministry of Defence and Serious Organised Crime Agency (SOCA). The MOD currently funds two members of the ADIDU.

Harmony guidelines on back-to-back tours identifying which trades are most at risk of having their harmony guidelines breached if the Afghanistan deployment is increased according to current plans

12. The Department's ability to achieve Harmony Guidelines, including separated service assumptions, is dependent upon the level of operational activity the Armed Forces are asked to undertake. Harmony is assessed as a trend over time using the time between operational tours—Tour Interval. Having taken into account present deployments in Iraq and the planned increase in deployments in Afghanistan, on average the Infantry, Royal Armoured Corps, Royal Artillery, Royal Engineers and Royal Signals will be approximately 20% deployed. An average of 20% deployed results in an average Tour Interval of 24 months—which is of course the "Harmony" target.

However, in 2006, as we increase our scale of effort in Afghanistan, tour intervals are likely to breach harmony levels in some areas such as medical, intelligence, helicopter crews, logistic, provost and engineers. We continue to encourage appropriate contributions from our NATO Allies in Afghanistan in order to take some of the pressure off these areas.

Overall, we judge that the impact on our planned deployment to Afghanistan and on readiness for future operations is manageable.

What has been the cost of Operation Herrick in Afghanistan in financial years 2002–03, 2003–04, 2004–05 and what is the projected cost for 2005–06 and 2006–07?

13. The total additional cost for the MOD's deployment to Afghanistan for 2004–05 was £67 million. The equivalent costs for previous years were: £311 million in 2002–03; and £46 million in 2003–04. We do not release the detail of projected figures they will be made available at the end of the financial year in accordance with standard MOD procedures. Overall we expect UK deployments in Afghanistan to cost around £1 billion over five years, commencing in the current financial year.

What is the MODs assessment of how effectively PRTs are extending the reach of the Afghan government beyond Kabul?

14. There is no fixed template for a PRT. Each is tailored to the prevailing security situation, socio-economic conditions, terrain, and reach of the Government of Afghanistan. Distinctions between the activities of PRTs are most obvious in relation to development, humanitarian and reconstruction activity. Generally, the UK does not support PRTs providing direct humanitarian assistance as this may lead to confusion about the PRT's primary role. However, the UK accepts that there may be areas of Afghanistan and situations in which this would be appropriate.

15. The UK PRT has successfully supported local disarmament initiatives, brokered by UNAMA, lobbied local factional leaders to engage constructively in the process, and monitored their compliance. Such initiatives have included the return of weaponry to arsenals while allowing the local non-militia population to register and keep personal weapons.

16. The PRT has played an active role in assisting the central government and the UK Ambassador in brokering solutions to local conflicts, including arrangement of cease-fires following clashes between militias in the north. The PRTs provide practical support from facilitating negotiations to providing transport to ensure the authority of the central government is reinforced during regional crisis.

17. The PRT has established good relations with NGOs active in its area. This has done much to dispel initial concerns from within the assistance community that the UK PRT would attempt to militarize development aid and blur the line between military and humanitarian activity. The PRT has made clear that it seeks neither to control nor co-ordinate development work. It does not task its military element with humanitarian assistance work. Instead, and through continuing dialogue and liaison with all regional actors, it seeks to facilitate the reconstruction effort. The DFID representative in the PRT has a fund to support a number of projects, all of which are carefully selected to avoid cutting across the core areas of work undertaken by NGOs, and to support the three basic objectives of the PRT. Activities funded have included a range of specific reconstruction projects including re-building police and judicial facilities, capacity-building of public institutions, a public library, and support for 700 poor families.

18. The UK PRT is increasingly becoming involved in police reform, recognising the risk of an accelerating Disarmament Demobilization and Reintegration process creating a security vacuum. This involvement has taken several forms. After a disarmament initiative in the Shulgareh Valley in August 2003, the PRT helped to support the local police force through the provision of basic equipment and continued mentoring. The PRT remains closely involved in supporting the 300 Afghan national policemen deployed from Kabul to Mazar-e Sharif in October 2003 to overcome the factional nature of the existing force. The UK funds five UK police advisers/mentors to work alongside US colleagues at the Regional Police Training College in Mazar. This has led to close liaison between the PRT, in particular the FCO and DFID representatives and police advisers, and local police authorities, to explore how the trained recruits might be most effectively deployed across the region. ANA and local police elements now routinely conduct joint patrols in the region. There is clear evidence to suggest that this action has reduced levels of banditry in previously notorious areas. It has also won the support of the local population, which clearly appreciates the effective presence of indigenous, centralised security institutions.

Which government department is responsible for activity in UK led PRTs? And how is the work of of MOD,DFID, FCO and civilian agencies co-ordinated?

19. The UK/ISAF PRT model is the first PRT to formalise the link between political, development and military actors. Effectively there is a joint command team comprising the PRT Commander (MOD), a Political Adviser (FCO) and a Development Adviser (DFID). This team are jointly responsible for activity in the PRT, and seek to integrate activities at an operational level. Each department is assigned lead responsibility for certain areas of work, to ensure that reporting lines, accountability and monitoring is effectively carried out. The Helmand PRT will see the MOD leading on most of the security related work, FCO leading on elements of governance and DFID leading on economic development.

What funds have been spent on development work in UK PRTs since 2003? What is the mixture of Government/ aid agency money spent on PRTs?

20. The UK PRTs have not undertaken development work; instead they work on stabilisation activities, which may be in the security, governance or development sectors, in order to enable a more permissive environment for development work to take place. DFID has been supporting the work of PRTs since 2003 through providing expert development advice to PRT command teams and supplying a small budget for quick impact development activities to the Development Adviser. To date DFID has spent approximately £2 million in this way. DFID funding to PRTs is currently one of the only sources of funding for PRTs to carry out quick impact activities.

The Government of Afghanistan do not deliver development assistance through PRTs; rather they employ implementing partners in the provinces. Similarly the aid community do not work directly with PRTs, and in many areas are not present in the environments in which PRTs work as a result of the security situation.

How do these funds compare to those spent in US controlled PRTs? What development money has been spent in Helmand province while under US control? Will this level of expenditure be maintained when Helmand PRT is the responsibility of the UK?

21. US PRTs have a different approach to stabilisation, focusing on explicit force protection or consent activities. Several pools of funding exist in US PRTs; these include US Commanders Emergency Response Program (CERP), USAID's QIP programme and the Defence Department's Overseas Humanitarian Disaster and Civic Aid Programme (OHDACA). Funding levels vary from PRT to PRT.

22. In Helmand province US CERP has spent some US$5.4 million, with an additional US$4.2 million allocated for existing projects and up to US$5.4 million more committed. USAID have allocated US$88.45m to Helmand for development activities over three years. The impact of US spend is uncertain and actual disbursement of US funds is lower than their allocation.

23. The UK plans to direct substantial funds to the Helmand province, mainly through other mechanisms than the PRT (primarily through the Government of Afghanistan's National Programmes, for labour intensive public works, small loans and rural infrastructure). A key difference will be that US spend to Helmand has concentrated on immediate and direct impact (not channelled through the GoA) whereas the UK will direct the vast proportion of our money through the government. This will help ensure international support is properly coordinated with Afghanistan's national development strategy and needs, and will also help to build the capacity of the GoA, thereby helping bring about conditions in which international forces can disengage.

14 February 2006

Third memorandum from the Ministry of Defence

Proposals put forward by the Senlis Council

1. As promised by Peter Holland, a copy of the 2001 report by David Mansfield (consultant), "An Analysis of Licit Opium Poppy Cultivation: India and Turkey" is attached.[51]

Will Reservists be deployed in Afghanistan? If so: how many, in which specialisms?

2. As announced by the Secretary of State on 26 January, the UK deployment to Afghanistan will comprise primarily regular troops. There will, however, be a small number of reservists, initially numbering up to around 100, drawn primarily from the Royal Rifle Volunteers (RRV) and 4th Battalion Parachute Regiment (4 PARA). A platoon from the RRV will undertake force protection tasks in Kabul, and officers

---

[51] See An Analysis of Licit Opium Poppy Cultivation: India and Turkey, by David Mansfield, Consultant, April 2001. Not printed.

and soldiers from 4 PARA will provide individual augmentation to the 3rd Battalion Parachute Regiment (3 PARA) as part of the UK Task Force. In addition there will be a number of logistics and medical personnel deployed with the UK Task Force, as well as a small number based at the ARRC and UK HQs in Kabul and Lashkah Gar.

What is MoD's assessment of the capability of the Afghan judicial system to dispense justice to any detainees handed over by ISAF forces?

3. Establishing the rule of law in any post-conflict situation presents a number of significant challenges. After 25 years of civil war and years of misrule by the Taliban regime, there were few recognisable elements of a rule of law process in place in Afghanistan. Progress since the conflict in 2001 has been slow, and Afghanistan's judicial sector capacity remains low. While some 60,000 police have now been trained and deployed, the necessary associated institutional reform of central ministries, and judicial reform more broadly, has failed to keep pace.

4. Efforts to resolve this are however underway. Italy continues to lead and co-ordinate international assistance in support of the Afghan Government's efforts, which, in 2005, coalesced around the Afghan Government's "Justice For All" strategy, and in 2006 the strong message in the Afghanistan Compact (launched at the London Conference on 31 January–1 February 2006) on the need for equal, fair and transparent access to justice for all. A UN Development Programme designed to support implementation of the "Justice for All" strategy has now been circulated to the international community, and the UK has agreed to provide $500,000 of seed funding to enable it to begin. This extensive programme seeks to accelerate the pace of judicial sector reform by: pursuing institutional reform of key central bodies such as the Ministry of Justice and Supreme Court; and seeking to improve the Afghan population's access to justice by developing the key infrastructure such as courthouses and prisons. Other initiatives, such as the Counter-Narcotics Criminal Justice Force, have seen progress with a number of successful prosecutions already made.

5. The UK is considering the capability of the Afghan authorities to receive and process any individuals handed over, including by making an assessment of local facilities, and based on the results of a recently concluded ICRC study of Afghan prison facilities. We are currently seeking to conclude a Memorandum of Understanding with the Government of Afghanistan that will stipulate not only UK expectations of the conditions in which the individuals will be held, but also that they will be subject to the due process of law. This matter is also being considered by NATO, in an attempt to develop a framework in which all ISAF forces can operate. The fundamental approach to detention remains that this should be Afghan-led, conducted by Afghan authorities, thereby avoiding the need for UK forces to detain individuals.

What pre-deployment training has been given to familiarise UK soldiers with the culture and conditions they will be experience in Afghanistan?

6. PJHQ and the three Front Line Commands conduct extensive training for all troops prior to deployment, designed to acclimatise them to the conditions and to hone their skills with procedures and equipment. Personnel deploying to Afghanistan have undergone training in various parts of the UK, which was designed to practise the infantry and vehicle skills required for the full spectrum of likely operations (Operation HERRICK EAGLE).

7. ***[52]

8. UK troops deploying also receive a mandatory pre-deployment training package which includes cultural awareness and basic language skills presentations, with handouts distributed to all personnel for easy reference. In addition, unit level training includes testing soldiers' ability to operate in replica theatre conditions, with Afghan nationals playing the role of the civilian population and interpreters. Additional higher level training was also delivered for commanders, including a presentation from Dr Sookhdeo (Director of the Institute for the Study of Islam and Christianity), a two day theatre Immersion package designed to promote a better understanding of the Afghan theatre, and a joint Inter Agency Multinational Training Day aiming to create an understanding of the capabilities and limitations of agencies operating in theatre. Underlying all these activities is a realisation that Afghanistan is a complex environment, that the consent of the people is a key factor and that this depends on our troops having an understanding of the Afghan people.

[52] Not printed.

Your memorandum of 14 February states that "the UK plans to direct substantial funds to the Helmand province". How much is "substantial"? What measurable outcomes is the UK seeking to achieve as a result of this spending?

9. The UK intends to disburse £38 million in the first year of full activity in Helmand. These funds will support activities in the fields of governance, economic and social development, security sector reform and counter-narcotics. The UK outline plan for its three-year deployment in Helmand contains benchmarks, milestones and foreseen outputs and outcomes, designed to build capacity of key provincial institutions, central line ministry representation, and thereby extend the reach of the central government.

10. At this initial stage of the deployment—the first wave of civilian staff arrived in the week beginning 20 March—it is difficult to be precise about measurable outcomes, but we would hope to see tangible improvements in, inter alia, opportunities for legal rural livelihoods, the capacity of the Provincial government, judicial system and security forces, and in the Governor's counter narcotics campaign. One of the first tasks of the civilians is to work with their military colleagues to test the outline plan and design the programmes required to deliver it.

Will UK Commanders have money available to fund small-scale local projects?

11. Funds for small-scale local projects will be available. But unlike in the US PRT model, these funds will be allocated by the PRT leadership triumvirate of the military commander, FCO political representative and DFID development adviser rather than automatically available to the UK Commander. This is due to the different approach taken by the UK to its PRTs. While the military component will be responsible for overall security, force protection and day-to-day operation of the PRT compound, wider PRT leadership reflects the multi-disciplinary approach of the UK, with a military, political and developmental triumvirate collectively guiding the PRT's interaction with local institutions and the local population.

12. The Lashkar Gah PRT will have access, as do other HMG representatives in Afghanistan, to the funds available in the Afghanistan Strategy of the Global Conflict Prevention Pool, designed to support creative and innovative projects to build long-term and sustainable capacity in security sector reform, prevent conflict, and develop a better understanding of local and regional power dynamics.

13. In addition, and recognising the need for rapid support to be delivered to the local Afghan institutions, the Lashkar Gah PRT will also have access to a Quick Impact Projects fund, designed to demonstrate the UK's support to Helmand, through short-term one-off projects or donations. Disbursement of the funds will be agreed on a trilateral basis between the military, FCO and DFID representatives, and overseen by the UK Regional Co-ordinator based in Kandahar, who will bring a regional perspective to this short-term activity.

16 March 2006

Memorandum from the Senlis Council

INTRODUCTION

1. The Senlis Council is an international think tank established by The Network of European Foundations; its initial focus on global drug policy has been broadened to encompass security and development. The Council convenes politicians, high profile academics, independent experts and Non-Governmental Organisations. It aims to work as the dialogue partner with senior policy-makers at the national and international levels in order to foster high-level exchanges and new ideas on bridging security and development.

2. The Senlis Council launched its policy initiative with respect to opium production demonstrating the centrality of the drug issue in Afghanistan's reconstruction process. The initial findings of the Council's *Feasibility Study on Opium Licensing in Afghanistan for the Production of Morphine and Other Essential Medicines* addressed the global shortage of opium-based medicines such as morphine and codeine, and ascertained the effects of licensed opium production in Afghanistan[53]. The Senlis Council is committed to conducting further in-depth research on the implementation of an opium licensed system for essential medicines. It has commenced field research activities in collaboration with international and Afghan experts providing further insight into the various aspects of opium licensing, mainly rural economics and local control mechanisms.

---

[53] The initial findings of the *Feasibility Study on Opium Licensing in Afghanistan for the Production of Morphine and Other Essential Medicines* spelled out a series of conclusions and recommendations for the implementation of a controlled licensed opium system in Afghanistan, which would function as a bridge between development and security in the country. Specialised contributions were given by The British Institute of International and Comparative Law; University of Calgary; University of Ghent; University of Kabul; University of Lisbon; University of Toronto; Wageningen University. 1st edition, September 2005; 2nd edition, November 2005; 3rd edition, January 2006.

DEPLOYMENT OF BRITISH TROOPS TO SOUTHERN AFGHANISTAN: AN OPPORTUNITY FOR A POSITIVE IMPACT ON THE REGION

3. The UK's deployment of 3,300 British troops to southern Afghanistan under NATO's operational plan for the ISAF mission to assist in the stabilisation and security efforts in the region represents a unique opportunity for the British forces to make a positive impact on the region and provide the secure environment in which the rule of law can be applied.

4. British forces in southern Afghanistan are faced with the twin mission of counter insurgency and support to counter narcotics. However, in a region where opium cultivation is deeply entrenched, the war against opium could make the war against insurgency a much more difficult, probably impossible, task. It is important that the fundamental stabilisation mission of British troops is not compromised by the war against opium.

5. British forces are urged to refrain from aggressive drug policies which undermine the livelihood of rural communities and fuel volatility. Instead, they should give support to development-based approaches, such as licensed opium production for essential medicines. In the fragile context of post-conflict Afghanistan, balancing the two objectives of security and development is the decisive factor in winning the "hearts and minds" of the Afghan people and contributing to Afghanistan's recovery.

6. Security and development are two inseparable sides of the reconstruction efforts in Afghanistan. And, crucially, opium lies at the core of the Afghan reconstruction nexus. According to the UNODC *Afghanistan Opium Survey 2005*, opium accounts for approximately 52% of the county's Gross Domestic Product with the net income from opium exports reaching US$2.7 billion. 309,000 households are involved in opium cultivation, representing 11.2% of the rural population.

7. Helmand is one of the main opium-producing Afghan provinces with opium cultivation accounting for more than 50% of the province's income in 2005, whilst UNODC predicts a staggering 50% increase in opium cultivation in the province for 2006. Importantly, illegal opium fuels a wild-fire economic development and opium resources are channelled into the criminal sector, insurgent and terrorist groups, thus creating a growing threat to the development of the rule of law in Afghanistan.

8. *Recommendation:* The mission of the British forces in southern Afghanistan with regards to opium should be clearly defined in order to avoid any clash with the primary mission of counter insurgency. The terms "support" to eradication activities can take many shapes on the ground and should therefore be defined in more specific detail beforehand. In a province which is increasingly falling into the grip of Taliban and other insurgent groups, it is vital British forces win the trust of local communities by avoiding to undermine their livelihoods. This can be achieved by giving precedence to a development-based approach in relation to the opium crop problem.

CURRENT DRUG POLICY APPROACHES IN AFGHANISTAN

9. The Senlis Council salutes the aid commitment of the United Kingdom to the area of counter narcotics in Afghanistan which reached over £50 million for the period 2003–05. Most particularly, The Senlis Council commends the Ministry of Defence and other government departments including the Foreign and Commonwealth Office and the Department for International Development on their commitment to provide £270 million over the next three years for Afghan counter narcotics activity.

10. However, current policies pursued in the area of counter narcotics have proven to be ill-adapted to the conditions and needs of local communities. A significant part of the UK financial commitment is poured into aggressive strategies, including crop eradication. Such forceful interventions primarily affect the most vulnerable actors of the opium economy—the farmers—destroying their livelihoods. Alternative development measures usually come after striving to mend the damage caused by such aggressive measures, however, failing to meet the immediate needs of farmers and of rural communities at large.

11. Despite deliberations regarding the progress made in curtailing opium cultivation in 2005, the total opium production in Afghanistan is estimated at around 4,100 tons representing a decrease of only 2% compared to the 4,200 metric tons harvested in 2004; a decrease which is, in fact, widely attributed to economic and weather conditions rather than to current counter narcotics activity. In addition, according to the UNODC *Afghanistan Opium Survey 2005,* record cultivation levels have been reported for nine Afghan provinces with the country's share of opium production remaining unchanged from 2004 at 87% of the world total.

12. The above provides clear evidence of the limited ability of current drug policies and specifically of crop eradication to influence opium cultivation and production in Afghanistan to any considerable degree. Unless development initiatives are endorsed as pre-condition to any drug intervention, insisting on current policies will continue failing to address the opium crisis in a comprehensive manner.

13. In light of the Afghan Government's weak capacity in implementing its counter-narcotics activity— only 30 police officers are reported to be trained in counter narcotic activities in the Province of Helmand, the support role of the British forces could, on the ground, shift towards direct engagement in counter-narcotics activity. Such a shift in the British forces' mission in southern Afghanistan towards direct military action against the drug stakeholders could lead to engaging in combat with those farmers who resist eradication.

This does not only conflict with NATO's operational plan for the ISAF mission but will, most importantly, compromise the stabilisation efforts of the forces in the region. Forceful action in the form of crop eradication will only spur discontent with the Government and fuel volatility, thus intensifying the security challenges facing British forces in the province.

14. *Recommendation:* Counter narcotics efforts in Afghanistan have, so far, proven largely ineffective in addressing this all-encompassing crisis—the illegal opium trade remains an impediment to sustainable development. British forces deployed in southern Afghanistan must refrain from endorsing current aggressive strategies which destroy the livelihoods of rural communities and compromise the conditions necessary for the establishment and good operations of the Provincial Reconstruction Teams (PRTs).

OPIUM: TURNING A THREAT INTO A DEVELOPMENT RESOURCE

15. The Afghan formal legal system provides a solid framework within which an opium licensing can be implemented. In particular, the new piece of Afghan legislation on drugs specifically referring to the production of opium (Chapter II, Articles 7 to 16) makes extensive provisions for the licensed cultivation of opium poppy for the production of morphine and other essential medicines. The new law, which was drafted with the assistance of the international community and particularly the UK and the US Governments, reflects the provisions on opium licensing laid down in the United Nations 1961 Single Convention on Narcotic Drugs, to which Afghanistan and 179 other countries are Parties.

16. According to the WHO there is a global pain crisis due to a shortage of opium-based essential medicines such as morphine and codeine despite the fact that a number of countries, including Turkey, India, France and Australia already grows opium for medicinal purposes under a strict licensing system. The International Narcotic Control Board has ascertained that seven of the richest countries –the United States, United Kingdom, France, Spain, Italy, Australia and Japan- consume nearly all of the world's supply of opium-based medicines, leaving 80% of the world's population with little or no access to these vital painkillers.

17. The opium licensing system is based on the comprehension that the opium issue is, at its core, one of economic resource management. If not properly managed and strictly controlled, opium could lead to instability and hinder long-term economic development. But by re-directing the opium poppy into the formal rural economy through the implementation of a strictly controlled opium licensing system, opium could become a major driver for a sustainable and diversified Afghan rural economy. In view of the world shortage of essential medicines, the development of an Afghan brand of morphine and codeine could also be endorsed. In particular, the distribution of Afghan morphine and codeine in neighbouring countries will also provide Afghanistan the opportunity to make a positive contribution to the region.

18. Opium licensing is a control system in itself generating the conditions necessary for the development of the rule of law. Initial findings of the Council's Feasibility Study reveal that an opium licensing system in Afghanistan will provide a sustainable and comprehensive response to the economic needs of farming communities; farmers cultivating opium under a licensing system will receive a steady and legally secure income equivalent to that which they currently receive for opium cultivated for the illegal heroin trade. Furthermore, traditional governance structures such as the *Jirga/Shura* and elders' assemblies could be integrated with formal state mechanisms and play a central role in enforcing and regulating an opium licensing system especially in remote areas where the Central Government has currently little or no control.

19. Supporting the implementation of an opium licensing system in provinces such as Helmand will work as a positive lever for British troops to win over the trust and support of local populations and to be associated more closely with reconstruction efforts instead of being regarded as a purely military force embarking on targeted forceful action against farmers and their families.

20. *Recommendation:* The UK, as a leading country in counter narcotics activity in Afghanistan, should consider re-directing the opium poppy—into the formal economy through the implementation of an opium licensing system rather than following the unrealistic goal of complete eradication. Opium licensing represents the opportunity to associate rural communities to reconstruction efforts rather than to alienate them through failing drug policy responses.

1 March 2006

Memorandum from Afghan Drugs Inter-Departmental Unit (ADIDU)

INTRODUCTION

1. Despite a 21% reduction in opium poppy cultivation in 2005 (130,000 hectares in 2003–04 to 104,000 hectares in 2004–05), the drugs trade remains a significant challenge to Afghanistan's long-term security, development and effective governance. It undermines stability of the region and accounts for almost 90% of the world supply of opiates.

2. The Afghan Government has, with support from the UK as key partner nation for counter narcotics, recently reviewed and updated its *National Drug Control Strategy*. The Strategy focuses on four key priorities: disrupting the drugs trade by targeting traffickers and their backers; strengthening and diversifying legal rural livelihoods; reducing the demand for illicit drugs and treatment of drug users; and developing effective state institutions to combat drugs at the central and provincial level.

3. We believe that focusing on these priorities will make a greater impact on the drugs trade and sustain the reduction in cultivation we have seen in 2005. But sustainable drug elimination strategies take time—particularly when the challenges are as severe as those in Afghanistan. The UK remains committed to the challenge and to supporting the delivery of the *National Drug Control Strategy*.

PROGRESS TO DATE

4. The London Conference on Afghanistan held on 31 January–1 February saw the launch of three key documents: the *Afghan Compact*, the *National Drug Control Strategy* and the *interim National Development Strategy*. In recognition of the serious threat that narcotics pose to the broader reconstruction of Afghanistan, counter narcotics is included as a cross-cutting theme in the *Afghan Compact* between the Afghan Government and the international community and in the interim *National Development Strategy*. The Afghan Compact includes high level benchmarks to measure progess in the counter narcotics effort. These benchmarks are underpinned by the more detailed planning in the *National Drug Control Strategy* and the interim *Afghan National Development Strategy*.

5. The UK has helped to establish and provide training for the *Counter Narcotics Police of Afghanistan (CNPA)*—the lead drugs law enforcement agency, headquartered in Kabul. The UK is also providing training for the *Afghan Special Narcotics Force (ASNF)*, an elite and highly trained force, equipped to tackle high value targets across the country. Since January 2004, the CNPA and ASNF have seized approximately 165 tonnes of opiates, destroyed an estimated 317 drugs labs and made a significant number of arrests. We are also working with the international community to recruit and train a counter narcotics *Criminal Justice Task Force (CJTF)* of Afghan investigators, prosecutors and judges to work with the Counter Narcotics Police, to be able to push through successful drugs investigations and prosecutions. There are currently 80 specially trained members of the CJTF. Since May 2005, there have been over 170 prosecutions resulting in over 90 individuals being convicted.

6. The UK is also funding a £12.5 million (US$22 million) *Institutional Development project* to strengthen the Ministry of Counter Narcotics and other counter narcotics institutions in Afghanistan. Two Deputy Ministers have now been appointed to support the Counter Narcotics Minister. We are also helping the Afghans to build up a viable economy and rebuild Afghanistan's infrastructure through National Programmes (Micro-finance, the National Rural Access Programme and the National Solidarity Programme), to help develop Alternative Livelihoods. Through these programmes 7,000 kilometres of secondary roads have been rehabilitated, helping farmers get their produce to markets, and nearly $50 million of micro-credit has been made available to 264,000 people to invest in legal livelihoods. Over 10,000 Community Development Councils have been elected and over $161 million has been granted for over 16,000 projects to rehabilitate irrigation and small scale infrastructure.

7. Furthermore, the UK has also funded the development of *five drug treatment centres*. We are working with the Ministry of Counter Narcotics to determine how best to support activity in this area following the completion of the United Nations Office on Drugs and Crime's survey on drug use within Afghanistan late last year. The survey identified 3.8% of the Afghan population as being drug addicts. We are also supporting the Poppy Elimination Programme by funding the salaries of Afghan staff charged with raising awareness of the illegality of the opium industry and monitoring Governor-led eradication in priority poppy growing provinces.

UK RESOURCES

8. The *Afghan Drugs Inter-Departmental Unit* (ADIDU), operating out of the Foreign and Commonwealth Office, was created in February 2005, following approval by the Prime Minister. The Unit's role is to co-ordinate the Whitehall effort on Afghan counter narcotics. Meanwhile, the *British Embassy Drugs Team* (BEDT) manages the UK's counter narcotics work in Afghanistan. They work closely with law enforcement and intelligence agencies to support the Government of Afghanistan in the implementation the *Afghan National Drug Control Strategy*. Both ADIDU and BEDT include staff from the Foreign and Commonwealth Office, HM Revenue and Customs, the Department for International Development, the Home Office and the Ministry of Defence. ADIDU is overseen by a Stakeholder Group. This Group is chaired by the Foreign and Commonwealth Office's Director for Afghanistan and South Asia Directorate and comprises one member, mostly at Director level, from each of the Stakeholder departments and the Cabinet Office.

9. In September 2005, the UK announced new *UK funding* to be spent on counter narcotics activity supporting the Afghan Government in the delivery of their *National Drugs Control Strategy*. In total, we will provide more than £270 million over the next three years (financial years 2005 06, 2006–07 and 2007–08). The Department for International Development will provide around £130 million of the funding,

which will be spent on rural livelihoods and institutional development. The rest will come from other government departments including the Foreign and Commonwealth Office, Ministry of Defence and the Home Office. A top priority for this funding will be targeting traffickers and disrupting the trade.

COUNTER NARCOTICS TRUST FUND

10. The *Counter Narcotics Trust Fund* has been created to bring counter narcotics funding on budget; give the Afghans greater ownership over this important agenda; and ensure that assistance is targeted as effectively as possible. The United Nations Development Programme will administer the Fund, which will ensure transparency and accountability.

11. At the London Conference on Afghanistan, several delegations, including the US (US$2 million), Sweden (US$2 million) and the UK (at least £30 million (US$52.9 million) announced contributions to the Fund. The UK commitment of £30 million includes an initial £10 million from our Afghan Drugs Inter-Departmental Unit and £20 million from the Department for International Development (DFID). These contributions added to those already committed by Australia, New Zealand, the EC and Estonia (US$1.5 million. US$338k, US$18.4 million and US$50k respectively), giving a total of US$77 million pledged so far.

CULTIVATION/PRODUCTION FIGURES

12. In November 2005, the UN Office on Drugs and Crime (UNODC) confirmed the *poppy cultivation and production figures for 2004–05* from their annual survey. UNODC reported a 21% reduction in poppy cultivation from 131,000 hectares (ha) in 2004–04 to 104,000 ha in 2004–05. These overall percentages, however, mask significant variations between provinces. For example, Nangarhar (-96%), Badakshan (-53%) and Helmand (-10%) saw the most significant decreases. But other provinces, such as Balkh and Farah, saw increases. The US Office of National Drug Control Policy (ONDCP) also publicly released its cultivation figures in November, which match those of UNODC.

13. UNODC also estimated that opium production in 2004–05 was around 4,100 metric tonnes (mt), a decrease of only 100 tonnes (2.4%) compared to 2004. Good weather and an absence of crop disease were responsible for a significant increase in yield in 2004–05.

14. While the UNODC and US figures were encouraging, we need to be cautious about the future. An early indication of this year's possible cultivation levels is reflected in the UNODC's *Rapid Assessment Survey*, which was released in March. The survey shows that overall cultivation levels are unlikely to decrease below 104,000 hectares in 2005–06. Trends indicate a possible increase in cultivation in 13 of 31 provinces (particularly in the south), a decrease in three, with 16 remaining stable. It seems that it is the areas where governance and access to livelihoods has improved where progress last year may have been consolidated. Whatever the overall cultivation figure this year, we need to build on these successes and ensure that the downward trend in cultivation is maintained in the long term.

LICENSED CULTIVATION

15. The Senlis Council has put forward a proposal to promote the licensing of Afghan poppy farmers to produce the raw materials for the manufacture of diamorphine and codeine in their *"Feasibility Study on Opium Licensing in Afghanistan for the Production of Morphine and Other Essential Medicines"*. The production of opium is contrary to Afghanistan's Constitution. The Afghan Government has expressed its opposition to *licit cultivation in Afghanistan*. When the Senlis Council presented its study in Afghanistan in September 2005, the Afghan Minister for Counter Narcotics, Habibullah Qaderi said, "The poor security situation in the country means there can simply be no guarantee that opium will not be smuggled out of the country for the illicit narcotics trade abroad. Without an effective control mechanism, a lot of opium will still be refined into heroin for illicit markets in the West and elsewhere. We could not accept this."

16. We share the view that licensing opium cultivation in Afghanistan is not a realistic solution to the problems of opium cultivation in Afghanistan, not least because it risks a high level of diversion of licit opium into illegal channels. It is clear from the feasibility study, as well as expert opinion that Afghanistan currently does not meet the prerequisites necessary to control licit cultivation. There is also a risk that prices would risk attracting new entrants into the illicit market.

Peter Holland
Foreign and Commonwealth Office

2 March 2006

ISBN 0-215-02828-7

9 780215 028280